VISIONARIES

IN URBAN DEVELOPMENT

15 Years of the ULI J.C. Nichols Prize Winners

Recommended bibliographic listing:
Riggs, Trisha, et al. *Visionaries in Urban Development: 15 Years of the ULI J.C. Nichols Prize Winners*. Washington, D.C.: Urban Land Institute, 2014.

Urban Land Institute
1025 Thomas Jefferson Street, NW
Suite 500 West
Washington, DC 20007-5201

ISBN: 978-0-87420-348-6

URBAN LAND INSTITUTE

The mission of the Urban Land Institute is to provide leadership in the responsible use of land and in creating and sustaining thriving communities worldwide. ULI is committed to

- Bringing together leaders from across the fields of real estate and land use policy to exchange best practices and serve community needs;

- Fostering collaboration within and beyond ULI's membership through mentoring, dialogue, and problem solving;

- Exploring issues of urbanization, conservation, regeneration, land use, capital formation, and sustainable development;

- Advancing land use policies and design practices that respect the uniqueness of both built and natural environments;

- Sharing knowledge through education, applied research, publishing, and electronic media; and

- Sustaining a diverse global network of local practice and advisory efforts that address current and future challenges.

Established in 1936, the Institute today has more than 32,000 members in more than 90 countries, representing the entire spectrum of the land use and development disciplines. ULI relies heavily on the experience of its members. It is through member involvement and information resources that ULI has been able to set standards of excellence in development practice. The Institute has long been recognized as one of the world's most respected and widely quoted sources of objective information on urban planning, growth, and development.

Patrick L. Phillips
Global Chief Executive Officer, ULI

CONTRIBUTORS

Principal Author

Trisha Riggs

Contributing Authors

Kathryn Craig
Steven Gu
Julianne Hill
Daniel Lobo
Archana Pyati
Beth Silverman
David Takesuye

Project Staff

Gayle Berens
*Senior Vice President, Education
and Advisory Group*

Daniel Lobo
*Project Manager
Director, Awards*

Kathryn Craig
Associate, Education and Advisory Group

Steven Gu
Intern

Trisha Riggs
Vice President, Communications

Adrienne Schmitz
Senior Director, Publications

Beth Silverman
Director, Education and Advisory Group

Archana Pyati
Impact Writer, Strategic Communications

Natasha Hilton
Associate, Education and Advisory Group

James A. Mulligan
Senior Editor

Christine Stinson, Publications
Professionals LLC
Manuscript Editor

Betsy Van Buskirk
Creative Director

Amy Elfenbaum and Kurt Wisthuff
Arc Group Ltd
Book Designers

Craig Chapman
Senior Director, Publishing Operations

CONTENTS

FOREWORD

The ULI J.C. Nichols Prize for Visionaries in Urban Development was established in 2000 to recognize a commitment to the highest standards of community building and to serve as a symbol of excellence in land use leadership that reflects both the mission of the Urban Land Institute and the values of the prize's namesake, ULI founding member Jesse Clyde Nichols.

> *"If J.C. Nichols were known only for his creation of the Country Club District and the Plaza, he would still be honored as a pioneer in quality real estate development. Yet his own vision was much broader. His intention was to make the city better, make his peers better professionals, and make the face of the nation better."*
>
> THE J.C. NICHOLS CHRONICLE: THE AUTHORIZED STORY OF THE MAN, HIS COMPANY, AND HIS LEGACY, 1880–1994

In the 15-year history of the Nichols Prize, we have celebrated extraordinary individuals: Joseph P. Riley Jr., mayor of Charleston, South Carolina; the late U.S. Senator Daniel Patrick Moynihan; Gerald D. Hines, founder and chairman of Hines; former Yale professor Vincent Scully; Richard D. Baron, chairman and chief executive officer of McCormack Baron Salazar; Albert B. Ratner, cochairman emeritus of Forest City Enterprises; Peter Calthorpe, founder and principal of Calthorpe Associates; Sir Stuart Lipton, partner at Lipton Rogers LLP; F. Barton Harvey III, former chairman and chief executive officer of Enterprise Community Partners; Amanda M. Burden, former commissioner of the New York City Planning Commission; former Chicago Mayor Richard M. Daley; His Highness the Aga Khan; Peter Walker, partner at PWP Landscape Architecture; J. Ronald Terwilliger, chairman emeritus of Trammell Crow Residential; and Dr. Judith Rodin, president of the Rockefeller Foundation (Rodin, the 2014 winner, is the 15th recipient).

These Nichols laureates are an elite group of leaders whose diverse backgrounds and areas of expertise illustrate the unique interdisciplinary nature of ULI. Whereas each recipient has profoundly affected community building in different ways, the characteristic they all share, which unites them and makes them very deserving of the Nichols Prize, is a deep understanding of how their work contributes to civic pride—the driving force behind communities that are cherished for generations. They recognize that thoughtful planning, design, and development play powerful roles in shaping how people feel about where and how they live. They know that great cities are made not of buildings, streets, and plazas, but of experiences and interactions that make great memories.

Through their actions and their accomplishments, these Nichols laureates have applied their skills in urban planning, design, development, teaching, and governing to create the best outcomes for our cities. But, most important, they are visionaries who have inspired others with their passion to make a positive, lasting impact. In this regard, they are carrying on the legacy of J.C. Nichols, whose commitment to excellence in ULI's early years continues to influence the 21st-century work of the Urban Land Institute in building a better world through better communities.

Patrick L. Phillips
Global Chief Executive Officer
Urban Land Institute

VISIONARIES

IN URBAN DEVELOPMENT

15 Years of the ULI J.C. Nichols Prize Winners

This volume celebrates the 15th anniversary of the Urban Land Institute's renowned recognition—the ULI J.C. Nichols Prize for Visionaries in Urban Development, named for my grandfather, J.C. Nichols. It provides profiles of the 15 remarkable recipients from 2000 through 2014, including the original article published during the year in which they were honored and an update on their current activities. What distinguishes each of these individuals is a shared commitment to improving the urban environment for future generations. It is a lofty goal that J.C. Nichols held steadfast even during the Great Depression when the business of building communities was practically nonexistent.

J.C. Nichols was one of the great real estate developers of the pre–World War II era, a person who knew that the act of building was also the act of creating community and who saw his mission as combining that larger calling of community with the quest for comfort and beauty. He understood that successful real estate development did not exist in isolation. And he understood that although a development must make economic sense, it also must make social sense and enrich the surrounding community. His guiding principles were "building for permanence" and "beauty is value added."

J.C. approached development as creating complete, interconnected communities. When he built homes, he considered all aspects of a person's life—art, culture, education, shopping, worship—and he incorporated them into his neighborhoods. In planning Kansas City's landmark Country Club District, J.C. sited homes, boulevards, parks, and other community components to enhance the existing terrain and natural landscape. J.C. required all homeowners to plant trees and shrubs on their properties. He established homeowners associations to sustain the neighborhoods he built and to keep homeowners accountable, instilling in them a sense of pride and belonging. In their support, he attended more than 75 homeowners association meetings annually.

In the early 1900s, J.C. Nichols and his peers would initiate the planning process through train trips in which they would visit each other, place their plans on the table, and help each other design master plans. Their goal was to create not just subdivisions or shopping centers but instead long-term, integrated planned communities. They said they viewed "land development as a responsibility, not a right."

Country Club Plaza, the iconic shopping center that Nichols built in 1922 in anticipation of the explosive popularity of the automobile, carried on the tradition of outstanding design. The plaza's Spanish motif, including several towers with intricate, colorful tile work, served to set off the shopping center and make it inviting. He did not want people just to come to shop; he wanted them to spend time there and enjoy being there. The role of the plaza as a community focus and "energizer" has remained constant through the years. Today, customs that were started in the 1920s—yuletide lights, an arts fair—still are favorites among Kansas City residents.

I remember my grandfather touring the district with me and his other grandchildren during the last years of his life and explaining his ideas to us. He understood the difference between simply building subdivisions connected by streets and utility lines and building neighborhoods connected by community events and shared amenities. Indeed, he never described his developments as subdivisions. J.C. believed that you must create the software of communities as well as the hardware. In this respect, he was very much a visionary. His imprint—giving the community an identity—is still alive. It is that sense of community—of togetherness—that still makes J.C. Nichols's work so important to community planning today.

> *"It is safe to say that J.C. Nichols would be proud to recognize his legacy in the work and ingenuity of these laureates. They come from different disciplines, with different approaches, but they all remind us that a proactive commitment to change is essential, that ideas and action go together."*
>
> WAYNE NICHOLS

The ULI J.C. Nichols Prize for Visionaries in Urban Development reflects the values shared by J.C. Nichols and ULI, as stated in ULI's mission, "to provide leadership in the responsible use of land and in creating thriving communities worldwide." The prize spotlights cutting-edge individuals or organizations that employ innovative processes, techniques, and insights in order to obtain the highest-quality development practices and policies. This prize is designed to encourage developers, planners, community leaders, and other related professionals to think profoundly about how urban development affects the livability of our neighborhoods. Our goal is for the prize to continue being a highly visible symbol focusing public attention on the importance of true visionary community development.

The Nichols Prize is funded by an endowment donated by the J.C. Nichols and Miller Nichols family. The presentation of the first ULI J.C. Nichols Prize for Visionaries in Urban Development in 2000 coincided with the 50th anniversary of the J.C. Nichols Foundation— now the ULI Foundation—which was created in 1950 by ULI trustees to perpetuate Nichols's ideals. In the 1940s, Nichols was instrumental in moving ULI forward by leading the establishment of the Institute's Community Builders Council (CBC). The council served as a forum in which industry professionals in the United States and Canada could exchange ideas and offer analyses of real estate practices. CBC meetings led to the publication of the *Community Builders Handbook*, written by Nichols and his peers throughout the country. It was the first authoritative publication on community planning and the forerunner to the subsequent ULI Development Handbook Series. The objectives of the CBC are carried out today by a wide range of specialized ULI councils.

The 15 years that have elapsed since the creation of the prize give us an opportunity to reflect and learn from a diverse group of laureates. These individuals and their organizations represent a broad array of disciplines, approaches, and contributions to making better places to live. It is safe to say that J.C. Nichols would be proud to recognize his legacy in the work and ingenuity of these laureates. They come from different disciplines, with different approaches, but they all remind us that a proactive commitment to change is essential, that ideas and action go together. Their contributions to helping communities succeed are the promise of an everlasting legacy that leads our actions for a better future.

The challenges and opportunities confronting future visionaries in urban development are as great or greater than those faced by J.C. Nichols and his fellow 20th-century community builders. The rapid expansion of digital technology and its effect on everyday life is the wild card in charting how to both renew and build anew the communities of the 21st century. The shifting social and cultural patterns emerging in response to the dramatic interconnectedness created by the digital revolution are only beginning to come into focus. It is the future visionaries who must translate these powerful new elements into livable, vital cities and meet the demands of an increasingly urbanized world.

Wayne Nichols
Santa Fe, New Mexico, August 2014

2000

Building on Success

Originally published in October 2000

Opposite: Waterfront Park's fountains. "Creating beautiful places for all citizens to own and enjoy is a moral imperative," Riley says. *(David McSpadden)*

It is an incredibly hot August day at Waterfront Park in Charleston, South Carolina, but the city's mayor, Joseph P. Riley Jr., is not fazed by the heat as he enthusiastically describes subtle features of the park that add to its overall aura of peacefulness. The reddish-brown gravel path between the lawn and the Cooper River is dense enough to accommodate wheelchairs, and the gravel's color is a pleasing transition from the park to the water, Riley points out.

The mayor knows this firsthand because he personally collected and inspected gravel samples to make certain the park's pathway was just right. He sketched the design for Waterfront Park's garden "rooms," which are several shaded areas, separated by small hedges, with benches for meditation, reflection, or simply relaxing. Riley made certain the park's stone border was just the right height (14 inches) to sit on or to serve as a footrest from nearby benches. It was his idea to install bench swings in covered pavilions on the park's pier. Riley rejected a proposal to ban children from splashing in the park's Vendue Fountain. And he insisted that all areas remain open to the public and never be closed, even partially, for private events.

For this visionary, the key to excellent urban development is to make every detail count and to create an atmosphere of inclusiveness, rather than exclusiveness. Joseph P. Riley Jr., mayor of Charleston for 25 years, feels a keen responsibility to let nothing fall through—especially in the design of public places.

"A city should be a place with such beauty and order that it is inspirational. A key component of urban design is a belief in the value of the public realm, which every citizen owns," he says. "If we are a nation where all the finest zones are privately owned, then what we own together as citizens is not very much. The greatest cities are those with the most beautiful public places, and that is what we've sought to achieve in Charleston."

It is this firm dedication to top-quality urban design for Charleston that led to Riley being selected as the first recipient of the ULI J.C. Nichols Prize for Visionaries in Urban Development. The $100,000 prize is named for the legendary Kansas City, Missouri, developer Jesse Clyde Nichols, a ULI founding member.

"A city should be a place with such beauty and order that it is inspirational. . . . The greatest cities are those with the most beautiful public places. There is no excuse for anything to ever be built that does not add to the beauty of a city."

JOSEPH P. RILEY JR. • 2000 NICHOLS LAUREATE

Left: Charleston City Art Gallery. *(Bill Murton, City of Charleston)*

Right: Charleston Place, the catalyst for the city's revival, features street-facing shops. *(Bill Murton, City of Charleston)*

A jury chaired by Robert C. Larson, managing director of Lazard Freres in New York City and chairman of the ULI Foundation, selected Riley for the Nichols Prize. "Mayor Riley's selection for the ULI J.C. Nichols Prize reflects his extraordinary contribution to Charleston's economic and social well-being," Larson says. "Through his leadership, Charleston has achieved an urban revival that sets the standard for many cities throughout the United States and demonstrates how the public sector and the private sector can work together to advance the common good."

Whether Riley is describing a grand hotel or a pump station, it is obvious that every development in Charleston must contribute to the community's values, spirit, and cohesiveness—the principles espoused nearly 100 years ago by J.C. Nichols.

"There is no excuse for anything to ever be built that does not add to the beauty of a city," Riley says. "Every investment in beauty yields an economic payoff. If you build beautiful places—whether they are parks, parking garages, or public housing—the land next to these places becomes more successful. They become catalytic agents to generate economic activity."

When Riley took office in 1975, Charleston's central business district was "essentially dead," he says. He and his advisers created a strategic plan for reviving the city, which included specific locations for hotels—all on main streets of the city, to "get people on the streets and generate activity," Riley says. The plan barred much development directly on the waterfront, because the goal was to encourage downtown growth but keep the city's waterfront open to the public. In fact, the 13 acres now occupied by Waterfront Park were slated for a commercial high-rise project. To keep the parcel accessible to the

Bench swings for adults on the Waterfront Park's pier.
(Bill Murton, City of Charleston)

public, the mayor arranged a land swap and pieced together financing to acquire the site for the park.

The first major hotel to spark Charleston's revival was Charleston Place, which, backed by a mix of public and private financing, opened in 1986. It is a magnificent, 442-room structure with grand chandeliers and sweeping staircases.

"We knew we were putting it (Charleston Place) in a sick part of town, but we also knew that if we got the right critical mass there, the area would come back to life," Riley says. Now, even in mid-August, when Charleston's steamy weather might hamper the city's tourism business, Charleston Place is booked solid. The bottom floor is filled with trendy retail shops and streets on either side are packed with specialty shops, gift shops, and eateries. The sidewalks are clean, wide, and inviting.

"You don't make a city beautiful just to attract visitors. If you make a city special for those who live there, then the tourists will come. When the people of Charleston come downtown, they come to a place they own, a place that gives them pride in their city," Riley says.

Charlestonian and ULI member John C. Darby credits Riley with two significant achievements: one being the revitalization of downtown. "He is a master at mobilizing public/private partnerships," says Darby, vice president of the Beach Company. In past years, Darby's firm worked with the city on downtown projects financed in part by Urban Development Action Grants from the U.S. Department of Housing and Urban Development. "Joe [Riley] knew how to get the biggest bang for the buck with those federal grants, how to leverage them to the fullest extent," Darby says.

Riley's second great achievement, Darby says, is the fact that he's held the office of mayor for 25 years. "Over the years, his focus has shifted from generating urban revitalization and more tourism to striking a balance between growth and preservation efforts. He has maintained a strong, diverse support base, Darby says.

Since Riley was first elected as Charleston's mayor in 1975, the city has achieved a substantial decrease in crime, revitalized its historic downtown district, increased its affordable housing stock, and experienced dramatic growth in its Spoleto Festival U.S.A., a world-class arts festival held each spring.

However, the success is not without side effects. Riley recently created a task force to examine the issue of downtown gentrification and to work on a solution to the problem of displacement of moderate-income residents and small businesses by more affluent, and sometimes absentee, owners. "With the economy going great guns, the pace of displacement has accelerated," says John Hildreth, a member of the gentrification task force and the southeastern director of the National Trust for Historic Preservation. "But he [Riley] took the right approach by creating a group to work together on this. He has an incredible ability to bring people together, to build consensus."

In addition to gentrification, another major challenge for Riley is managing the area's growth, including a proposed expansion of the city's port. The city council rejected the original terminal construction proposal as simply too large, straining area roads with increased truck traffic. Instead, council members are seeking a smaller project. "This is a city where scale is everything, and we felt the original expansion plan was not the appropriate scale," Riley says.

Years ago, the mayor convinced Charleston citizens to approve a local sales tax to help bring in much-needed revenue for economic development and public projects. As the area's economy strengthened, real property values rose (Charleston's median home price rose from $74,500 to $131,700 between 1989 and 1999), and the city's property tax rate was reduced, as the reduction was offset by the sales tax revenue. This November, the city's residents will vote on a referendum to increase the sales tax by one-half of a penny, with the revenue going for development rights acquisition and land acquisition to give permanent protection to some of Charleston's prized farmland, marshes, and forests.

"Controlling sprawl does not mean stopping growth," Riley says. "A no-growth policy is bad public policy, because it leads to pent-up demand that explodes sooner or later. Controlling sprawl means strategically shaping growth. If we don't do that, then we are giving a nation of diminished value to our great grandchildren."

Part of Charleston's overall growth plan is based on direct input from its younger residents. Recently, city planners visited area schools to discuss plans for new development. "The kids talked about not being able to ride their bikes to visit schoolmates because a big road separated them from other neighborhoods. They said they couldn't ride up to a corner store, because there was no corner store," Riley says.

Daniel Island, one of several outlying areas annexed by the city, is being developed as a new urbanist community. It's designed as a total community with corner stores serving

Opposite:

Top: Riley leads the "Get in Step" march to remove the Confederate flag from the South Carolina State House. *(Bill Murton, City of Charleston)*

Bottom right: The city controls the number of horse-drawn carriages to protect nearby residential neighborhoods. *(Bill Murton, City of Charleston)*

Bottom left: The famous pineapple fountain—an immediate icon for the city. *(Bill Murton, City of Charleston)*

"*Through Mayor Riley's leadership, Charleston has achieved an urban revival that demonstrates how the public sector and private sector can work together to advance the common good.*"

ROBERT C. LARSON ▪ 2000 JURY MEMBER

Even the drainage pump station on the edge of downtown is designed as an outstanding civic project. *(Bill Murton, City of Charleston)*

nearby homes, with sidewalks and green strips connecting the entire project. "We felt we should focus on the qualities of new urbanism that we celebrate in downtown Charleston," Riley says.

According to Dana Beach, executive director of the South Carolina Coastal Conservation League, Riley's support of the development on Daniel Island illustrates his desire to restructure growth in an environmentally, fiscally sound manner. "Our challenge is to translate what we know about functional neighborhoods, based on what we've learned from downtown, and apply that to suburbs that are not yet fully developed," Beach says. "If anyone can do this, Joe Riley can. He's a visionary to be sure; but more important, he sees his vision through to reality."

Howard Duvall, executive director of the Municipal Association of South Carolina, describes Riley as a "worker, not a glad-hander" with no fear of taking political risks. "He'll get right in the middle of a debate and then do what he feels is best for the city," Duvall says.

While many mayors share Riley's passion for sound urban planning, few have his extensive knowledge of the design process, notes ULI senior resident fellow William H. Hudnut III, a former mayor of Indianapolis and a former member of the U.S. Congress. "Mayor Riley knows how cities are glued together by streets, parks, and businesses. His understanding of urban design is unusual for many mayors," Hudnut says.

SINCE RECEIVING THE NICHOLS PRIZE IN 2000

Charleston Mayor Joseph Riley has continued to serve with energy and passion in his tenth term as mayor.

After being recognized as the first Nichols laureate, Riley has continued to collect accolades and achievements. In 2002, the American Architectural Foundation awarded him the Keystone Award for exemplary leadership that has transformed communities through architecture and design. *Governing* magazine named him Public Official of the Year in 2003 for leveraging the power of urban design and civic space. He received the American Society of Landscape Architects Olmsted Medal in 2004 and the South Carolina Governor's Award in the Humanities in 2005. And in 2009, President Barack Obama presented Riley with the National Medal of Arts for cultivating Charleston's historic and cultural resources to enhance public spaces and for revitalizing urban centers throughout the nation as founder of the Mayors' Institute on City Design.

Among his many projects, Riley has worked tirelessly to see that the International African American Museum is built in Charleston Harbor. Charleston played a pivotal role during the slave trade, with four of ten slaves that arrived by ship passing through the city. "It's a profound opportunity to honor the African Americans who were brought here against their will and helped build this city and helped build this country," he told Charleston's *Post and Courier* newspaper. An estimated $75 million project, plans call for funding to come from private donations, the city of Charleston, and the state of South Carolina. If funds are procured by 2016, the museum is expected to open by 2018.

Though Riley has said he will not run for reelection in 2015, a decision he calls sound and irrevocable, he undoubtedly will continue to inspire Charleston and other municipalities for years to come. ∎

ULI leader Harry Frampton III, president of East West Partners in Beaver Creek, Colorado, is very familiar with Riley's design expertise. East West Partners is developing a residential condominium project next to Charleston's Waterfront Park. During a recent meeting to review plans, Frampton was surprised to see the mayor kneeling over the blueprints, studying every detail. "Mayor Riley was involved in the discussions on hardware, window designs, and colors, and he made suggestions for improvements, many of which we adopted," Frampton says. "Our company has worked in a lot of cities, but I've never seen a government official get so involved in the essence of a project. He was very concerned about how the units would look not just when they were finished, but 30 years from now. That is impressive."

A former president of the U.S. Conference of Mayors, Riley was a founder of the Mayors' Institute on City Design. The institute, which has assisted mayors from more than 100 communities, provides advice through panels of sociologists, municipal planners, traffic engineers, and landscape architects. "We [mayors] needed a place where mayors could become familiar with how urban design works," Riley said. "Mayors have a lot of influence over development in their communities, but they rarely have training in urban design. Yet, when they leave office, the development that occurred when they served is how they are remembered."

Riley will be remembered for many projects. The city's latest completed work, the $69 million South Carolina Aquarium, opened last May and expects up to 1 million visitors by the end of its first full year of operation. First proposed by the mayor in the 1980s, it features the aquatic environment of the entire state, from river otters in the mountains to moon jellies in the ocean.

"What we're doing in Charleston is creating places that give people wonderful memories," Riley says. "The idea is to give citizens pride in their communities by creating places that give them a sense of ownership, of belonging. That is the true American Dream."

2001

DANIEL PATRICK MOYNIHAN

Public Architecture's Political Agenda

Originally published in October 2001

Opposite: The 2.7 million-square-foot Ronald Reagan Building and International Trade Center opened in 1998, completing the redevelopment of Pennsylvania Avenue in Washington, D.C. *(Tim Hursley)*

Daniel Patrick Moynihan, the 2001 winner of the ULI J.C. Nichols Prize for Visionaries in Urban Development, is widely regarded as one of the nation's foremost authorities on urban planning and design. His commitment to sound urban development, which spans more than 40 years, includes service as a counselor for urban affairs to President Richard M. Nixon and cabinet-level or subcabinet-level positions in four presidential administrations, starting with the Kennedy administration in 1961. At that time, he already was well known as a leading expert on urban problems, and President John F. Kennedy asked him to draft a proposal to revitalize Washington's Pennsylvania Avenue.

Moynihan's proposal to President Kennedy recommended, "Care should be taken not to line the north side with a solid block of public and private office buildings that close down completely at night and on weekends . . . . Pennsylvania Avenue should be lively, friendly, and inviting, as well as dignified and impressive." This report led to the creation by Congress in 1972 of the Pennsylvania Avenue Development Corporation to implement the avenue's revitalization. Over the years, Moynihan's strong role in the revitalization of Pennsylvania Avenue and the surrounding area resulted in the rehabilitation of the Old Post Office Building, the Willard Hotel, and Union Station; the conversion of the old Pension Building into the National Building Museum; the construction of the Ronald Reagan Building and International Trade Center; and the construction of plazas and monuments, including the Western Plaza and the Navy War Memorial.

Moynihan represented New York in the U.S. Senate from 1977 through 2000. Known as the "architectural conscience" of Congress, he waged a tireless effort on public building and public works design that focused on planning before spending, saving old buildings worth saving, building new structures worth building, and moving ahead with projects rather than blocking them. He had no patience for what he considered ugly or boring. For example, in 1981, he introduced a Senate resolution to "put the plastic covering back on" the newly finished Hart Senate Office Building, describing the structure as a "building whose banality is exceeded only by its expense."

"The point about public space is that it is public. And people who own nothing much in their own right have a part of that [space]. The notion of civitas, of a citizen, of a person with a right and a responsibility to be there and participate in a public space: that is what it means to be a republic."

DANIEL PATRICK MOYNIHAN • 2001 NICHOLS LAUREATE

Top: Moynihan pursued the re-creation of a grand, above-ground Pennsylvania Railroad Station in New York City.

Bottom: The National Building Museum, in the former U.S. Pension Building, is "probably the greatest interior space in the Western Hemisphere," according to Moynihan. *(National Building Museum)*

While in the Senate, Moynihan ensured that federal empowerment zones were created by the Omnibus Budget Reconciliation Act of 1993 to provide tax benefits to economically disadvantaged areas nationwide. As the Senate sponsor of the landmark Intermodal Surface Transportation Efficiency Act (ISTEA) of 1991, he helped change federal rules to allow money to be spent on highway or public transit projects according to local needs. ISTEA requires policy makers to consider all transportation options, gives citizens the opportunity to participate in the planning process, and allows local agencies to be flexible in choosing how funds are spent.

Moynihan's priorities for New York City included the re-creation of a grand, above-ground Pennsylvania Railroad Station; the restoration of the Alexander Hamilton U.S. Custom House building in Battery Park; and the redesign of Foley Square. In Buffalo, he led efforts to restore the Prudential Building, designed by architect Louis Sullivan, and the National Guard Armory.

He still is pursuing the Penn Station project, which has yet to begin. In 1999, when the project was announced, Moynihan said, "It is up to a new generation to renew our cities. Penn Station is the start, and we will we complete this project—that suddenly all will seem possible. We are at the hinge of history, and you must push."

According to Paul Goldberger, Nichols Prize jury member and architecture critic for the *New Yorker* magazine, Moynihan understands the correlation between excellent building design and the economic and social stability of urban areas. "Pat Moynihan is one of the few people in national public life today who really respond to architecture, who take incredible joy and delight in great buildings, who know that great cities are made up not only of great individual buildings, but of wonderful places—streets, public squares, train stations—in which we live our public life together," Goldberger says. "He has always understood that a better physical environment can make life more satisfying, and he has done an incredible job in making the federal government a force behind good architecture and better cities. He unites the strands of political action and knowledge of the political system with architectural passion . . . . It's the miracle recipe for getting things done."

Last July, Moynihan shared his insights on urban development during an interview in the Woodrow Wilson Center for Scholars, located in the Ronald Reagan Building, which opened in 1998 as the final major project completing the redevelopment of Pennsylvania Avenue. His office is located in the 2.7 million-square-foot structure, which replaced what for years had been an 11-acre parking lot of "surpassing ugliness," as Moynihan once described it. Today, as the former senator walks to work from his apartment a few blocks away on the avenue, he sees his vision as reality: a "lively, friendly, inviting, dignified, and impressive" corridor worthy of being America's Main Street.

J.C. Nichols's neighborhoods were cohesive and built for performance to help create a sense of community. What is the connection between thoughtful urban design and the economic and social well-being of our cities?

MOYNIHAN: What J.C. Nichols did in Kansas City was to create a public space where people could walk about and be social. That is what we lost in cities with factories and no room for anything but manufacturing. Then, with the coming of the automobile, cities emptied out. Look at Washington: 40 years ago, Pennsylvania Avenue was abandoned. We're in the Woodrow Wilson Plaza in the Reagan Building, in what used to be a parking lot, where people come in, do what they have to do in Washington, and get out. Today, it's a plaza with bands, entertainment, people, and restaurants. In the redevelopment of Pennsylvania Avenue and of downtown Washington, we have discovered that people want to walk, like to gaze, and like to dine outside. The redevelopment has succeeded.

Time magazine cover, July 28, 1967, identifying Patrick Moynihan as an "urbanologist."

In general, is the design of our urban areas better now than 30 years ago? During the planning process, is more thought being given to ways to bring people together?

MOYNIHAN: Our cities are recovering from the trauma induced by the interstate highway system. [In 1956, the Federal Aid Highway Act authorized $24.8 billion for the construction of 40,000 miles of an interstate highway system. The system was completed 35 years later at a cost exceeding $125 billion.] The maps showed it connecting one city with another, but most of the funds for the program were spent in cities, and it destroyed them. One strategy that the engineers instinctively pursued was that if there was an open space, they covered it with an interstate. Open space just disappeared in our cities—not entirely, but enough so that the highway took you out of the city and there was nothing to bring you back. Today, that way of thinking is over. [In an article titled "New Roads and Urban Chaos," which he wrote for *Reporter* magazine in 1960, Moynihan predicted that interstates would drain people out of cities.]

ISTEA was a radical departure from traditional federal transportation policy. Are cities using the funding flexibility of ISTEA to help provide more transportation alternatives?

MOYNIHAN: With ISTEA, we said, "Enough highways; now let's get to other modes of transportation that are friendly to cities." Numbers of rail passengers are up, and public transit use is up, and the people [at the local level] who have the [planning and spending] authority under the legislation we passed like it. It's about regional planning—not just a group of graduate students coming down and telling other people what to do. It involves planning by persons who are part of the political infrastructure of the metropolitan areas. They say ISTEA is working and want it to stay.

Do other types of federal programs exist that can be used to help reverse sprawl and improve urban land use planning?

MOYNIHAN: Federal programs are problematic when it comes to cities. You can't run cities from Washington; when you try, it does not work. The first great effort was urban renewal. It definitely had successes. But it also produced great swaths of empty, knocked-down neighborhoods where other things were supposed to spring up, but didn't, because the Interstate Highway System simultaneously was sending the message, "Come on, it's great out here [in the suburbs]." So, we lost a lot of community in that process.

Is it realistic, then, to expect more federal support, perhaps even more funds, to assist cities in their redevelopment efforts?

MOYNIHAN: More federal funds means more federal instructions, regulations, and rules. I would say the present balance [of federal, state, and local funding] is about right, particularly when there is so much energy at the city level, which has not always been the case. There are urban advocates in Congress—anyone elected to the House of Representatives from a city or to the Senate from a state with a lot of cities is an urban advocate. What was not on our agenda 50 years ago is very much on our agenda today.

"Pat Moynihan is one of the few people in public life who really respond to architecture, who take incredible joy and delight in great buildings, who know that great cities are made up of wonderful places in which we live our public life together."

PAUL GOLDBERGER • 2001 JURY MEMBER

Are our cities adequately preparing for the population growth and demographic changes in the years ahead? What is the biggest challenge they face?

MOYNIHAN: We will not likely see the population explosions we've had in intervals over the past two centuries. Nowadays, our population growth is very reasonable and manageable. To be sure, there will be some areas, such as southern California, where it will be conspicuously heavier, but in the main, we've got a stable population, and we have suburbanized, so the inner cities will be able to accommodate those moving in. They are ready for redevelopment. Look at Manhattan. When I was growing up there, there was nothing between Wall Street and Greenwich Village. Houston Street was a big street with nothing but empty buildings, decrepit factories, and a few department stores where no one shopped. Today, it's the hottest real estate market in Manhattan, with young couples and individuals moving in. First, there was SoHo, then Tribeca, and now people are moving over to the waterfront, which used to be abandoned. They want to be in the city, and they want a city that is full of people. It is a cumulative process, but it obviously works. The biggest problem our cities have now is finding an attractive way for families to form and to grow. One of the reasons we fled our cities was to find a place where we could raise children. This problem is of more consequence than you might think.

In terms of the architecture of public buildings, has the public sector learned from its mistakes?

MOYNIHAN: When the city of Washington was designed, we had the Capitol, the White House, and the Treasury Building. Halfway between, the Old Patent Office—considered one of the purest examples of Greek Revival architecture in the United States—was built. It was about as fine a building as we've ever put up. In the 1950s, a bill was introduced in the Senate to knock that building down and sell it to a private developer for the construction of a parking garage. That means you've lost all memory of the principle that Thomas Jefferson put forth, which is that political thought and design activity are inseparable. A parking garage in the place of that wonderful building is a form of political thought we can do without. [The building was acquired by the Smithsonian Institution and avoided destruction.]

Penn Station in New York is another example of how architecture disappeared from our calculations. In the early 1960s, with the growth of interstate highways, everyone just "knew" that passenger rail was finished. By then, the Pennsylvania Railroad had been

SINCE RECEIVING THE NICHOLS PRIZE IN 2001

Daniel Patrick Moynihan and his work have continued to influence the built environment through a legacy that lives on. Moynihan, who died in 2003 at age 73, is sorely missed in the halls of Congress and within the architecture community. "Not since Thomas Jefferson has there been a public official who so understood architecture as well as Daniel Patrick Moynihan," architecture critic Paul Goldberger said at a symposium celebrating Moynihan's life that was sponsored by the American Institute of Architects and the U.S. General Services Administration.

In a tribute to Moynihan shortly after his death, then-ULI President Richard Rosan said, "Daniel Patrick Moynihan understood that worthwhile endeavors take a long time—that city building and rebuilding is a task that must withstand multiple changes in political administrations. The revitalization of Washington's Pennsylvania Avenue, which he conceived in 1962, was not completed until 1998—an undertaking stretching through eight presidential terms. Throughout his own 23-year term in the Senate, he never set aside his long-range view of urban issues in favor of "quick-fix" pursuits he could parade before voters in his next election. Rather, he focused on public building and public works projects that emphasized planning before spending, saving buildings worth saving, building new ones worth building, and moving ahead rather than stalling."

After declining to seek a fifth term in the U.S. Senate, Moynihan served as a senior policy scholar at the Woodrow Wilson International Center for Scholars in Washington, D.C., and joined the faculty at Syracuse University's Maxwell School of Citizenship and Public Affairs. His commitment to public service remained steadfast. Moynihan was appointed by then-President George W. Bush as cochair of the President's Commission to Strengthen Social Security and was a member of the National Commission on Federal Election Reform. After his death, Syracuse, using a $10 million grant from the federal government, created the Moynihan Institute of Global Affairs within the Maxwell School to honor the late senator and university professor.

In 2003, then-Governor George Pataki and U.S. Senator Charles Schumer proposed naming a redeveloped Pennsylvania Station in New York City "Moynihan Station" to honor the late senator, who long championed a plan to expand and rebuild the train station in the neighboring James Farley Post Office building and who proclaimed that the new development would be an "architectural masterpiece." Redevelopment plans are in place, with the first phase of Moynihan Station expected to be completed by 2016.

"His life was a testament to the fact that one man, who just thinks, can make an enormous difference," said Schumer, who served New York state alongside Moynihan in the U.S. Senate. "I just hope God gives us a few more Pat Moynihans in this Senate, and in this country." ■

President Richard Nixon and Moynihan on a walking tour of Pennsylvania Avenue in September 1970. *(Corbis Images)*

acquired by another railroad, which was interested in freight. They [the railroad owners] decided that they could make money by tearing down Penn Station [in 1963] and putting up hotels and Madison Square Garden, and they built a little hole for a station. Far from disappearing, rail traffic has gone up, and that little hole is headed for a calamity. Oh, how I remember that triumphant building! When you came up those steps from the track level, and entered that room, you knew you were in a great place. You felt like a great person. Tearing it down was a barbarous act. Right after, the city created the Landmarks Preservation Commission, one of the first "don't-touch-that-building" agencies in the country. [Since its creation in 1965, the commission has designated more than 1,070 individual landmarks, 77 historic districts, nine scenic landmarks, and 103 interior landmarks in New York City.] We've come a long way since then. When the new Penn Station is built, it will be an architectural masterpiece.

Now that the redevelopment of Pennsylvania Avenue in Washington has been completed, are you pleased with the way it has turned out? Is there anything you wish had been done differently?

MOYNIHAN: I wish the FBI Building had been done differently, but the plan for it already was set when we started working on the redevelopment proposal. In the original plan, J. Edgar Hoover wanted to be able to drive into the building and have an elevator take him—and his car—up to his office. Fortunately, the car elevator did not happen. We did get an agreement to move the building back so that there would be a wider sidewalk, and trees were planted in front of it. The [Pennsylvania Avenue] site for the Newseum is just about finished, and this very successful enterprise will be moving across the street from the west wing of the National Gallery of Art. Then, there is the National Building Museum, which is doing wonderfully in the old Pension building, which is probably the greatest interior space in the Western Hemisphere.

You have said that architecture in public buildings reflects the political values of a particular era and the competence of government. Does this hold true in society today?

MOYNIHAN: Absolutely. Look at what people do when they travel. They go from one country to another, from one continent to another, and mostly they go to look at buildings and to be in places that are congenial. The point about public space is that it is public. And people who own nothing much in their own right have a part of that [space]. The notion of *civitas*, of a citizen, of a person with a right and a responsibility to be there and participate in a public space: that is what it means to be a republic.

AMERICA'S MAIN STREET

Moynihan's Trojan-horse proposal for Pennsylvania Avenue went far beyond recommendations for new office space.

When Daniel Patrick Moynihan joined the new administration of President John F. Kennedy as a political appointee in 1961, he was one of the youthful and idealistic Whiz Kids that Kennedy had attracted to his administration. Moynihan already had established a reputation as a politically inclined intellectual and a student of urban issues. He had worked almost four years as an assistant to Governor Averell Harriman of New York, and he had taught two years at Syracuse University, researching the sociology of urban life. But he was not an insider within the Kennedy circle, and his first assignment was as special assistant to Secretary of Labor Arthur Goldberg. To Goldberg, Kennedy assigned the task of improving Pennsylvania Avenue's dilapidated image, a condition that Kennedy noticed during his inaugural parade from the Capitol to the White House, a route every president since Thomas Jefferson has taken following the ceremonial oath of office. For that task, Goldberg called in his head of research, Daniel Patrick Moynihan.

In his inaugural speech, President Kennedy spoke of an America—of a world—full of challenges and potential. America was on the verge of a New Frontier, he declared, and his fateful challenge exhorted Americans to "ask not what your country can do for you—ask what you can do for your country." Through this prism—rose-colored, perhaps—the young functionaries and the veteran politicos in the executive branch saw each task of government as an unbounded appeal to the generous paternalism of big government. Moynihan, like Kennedy, was young, Irish-Catholic, and a veteran of the Navy; and he was in lockstep with the president's idealism.

Some two centuries earlier, Major Pierre Charles L'Enfant had conceived a plan for the new federal capital city that was to be a masterstroke of grand design tempered with realism and pragmatism. Chosen by President George Washington, the ten-mile-square district—comprising swamps, creeks, woodlands, and rural pastures—straddled the Potomac River and included four settled towns. Avoiding these communities and choosing Jenkin's Hill

A model of L'Enfant's plan for Pennsylvania Avenue is displayed at Freedom Plaza. *(Tom Bernard/Courtesy of VSBA)*

(now Capitol Hill) as the locus for public buildings, L'Enfant, schooled in French academies and borrowing from his native Versailles, oriented a grand vista westward, expressing the nation's manifest destiny. Crossing this major axis at a perpendicular was a minor axis, at the northern end of which L'Enfant placed the President's House. The resulting mile-long hypotenuse—named Pennsylvania Avenue as a concession to the runner-up state in the sweepstakes to host the federal district—connected the executive branch of the government with its legislative counterpart. This physical and symbolic link held special significance in L'Enfant's plan of rational grids overlaid with Baroque-like radiating boulevards. These ceremonial axes have been maintained, except that the Washington Monument was shifted slightly off the north–south White House axis, and the Treasury Building blocks the view of the Capitol building from the White House.

Pennsylvania Avenue, by default, became the new capital city's main commercial street. The 70-acre triangle formed by the Mall to the south and Pennsylvania Avenue to the north was populated with commercial establishments and was considered a seedy part of town at that time. Fueled by the growth of government after World War I, the drive to spruce up the Federal Triangle culminated in 1928 with the federal government's purchase of all the land within the triangle; the construction of uniform, neoclassical buff-colored limestone buildings for various departments and agencies of the government; and the elimination of 23 of L'Enfant's original city blocks.

Meanwhile, the north side of Pennsylvania Avenue was suffering a similar decline. The Great Depression caused the closing of many businesses, and as commercial activity on the avenue dwindled, the remaining businesses found better markets elsewhere in the city or, increasingly, in the suburbs.

This was the Pennsylvania Avenue that newly inaugurated President Kennedy reviewed from his car when he paraded down the "Avenue of the Presidents" in January 1961, and that Moynihan was asked to do something about. At least, that is the apocryphal version. How Moynihan came to be so closely associated with Pennsylvania Avenue's redevelopment is more captivating than legend. It was Goldberg, Moynihan's mentor, who actually noticed the sad state of "America's Main Street." Mary Cable quotes Goldberg in *The Avenue of the Presidents* (Boston: Houghton and Company, 1969):

"It was the day of Kennedy's inauguration. Each cabinet officer had a car, and rode . . . down Pennsylvania Avenue. I found it a

Pennsylvania Avenue during John F. Kennedy's inaugural parade in January 1961. *(Courtesy of the History Place)*

moving experience and could not help but be concerned about the contrast between the grandeur of the occasion and the shoddy street. On one side of it we have a phalanx of mammoth government buildings . . . . On the other, old buildings of no architectural worth. And yet the Avenue is the physical link between the Executive and the Congress. To me, the neglect of the Avenue demonstrates the neglect of a basic problem and a failure of government. How can government function in a decaying, declining city?"

In their book, *Pennsylvania Avenue: America's Main Street* (Washington, D.C.: The AIA Press, 1988), Carol Highsmith and Ted Landphair quote Goldberg's description of the Avenue as consisting "of a bunch of decrepit pawn shops, taverns, horrible souvenir shops that took advantage of tourists, and secondhand clothing stores. In sum, it was a disgrace." (Kennedy later agreed with this description, saying he and his wife shared Goldberg's "dismay over the ramshackle appearance of the nation's ceremonial street.")

Also recounted in *Pennsylvania Avenue* is a recollection by Robert Peck, a former aide to Moynihan and a past commissioner of the Public Buildings Service at the General Services Administration. Moynihan "turned a cabinet meeting which was mainly bitching about parking in federal buildings—all right, it was supposed to be about office space, but it was also about parking, it always is—and he turns that into 'Guiding Principles for Federal Architecture'!" Peck also is quoted as commenting, "Moynihan is so loyal to the memory of John F. Kennedy that he still insists it was Kennedy's idea to fix up Pennsylvania Avenue."

In any event, it became Moynihan's task to prepare a report to the president on behalf of the ad hoc committee; the 62-page report on federal office space utilization was released in June 1962. Two illuminating appendices to the report summarized Moynihan's thinking on the subject of the government's role in urban planning and policy, presaging his continuing interest in these issues over the years since, both in official and unofficial capacities.

The first appendix is the one-page, unsolicited treatise "Guiding Principles for Federal Architecture," referred to by Peck. In it, Moynihan writes as if he were delivering his raison d'étre for government service: the federal government's architectural policy should call for "an architectural style and form which is distinguished and which will reflect the dignity, enterprise, vigor, and stability of the American national government." Its buildings should "reflect the finest contemporary American architecture, incorporating fine art, such as sculpture and murals." With a glance at the homogeneity of the neoclassical Federal Triangle, Moynihan wrote, "the development of an official style must be avoided."

The second appendix is equally stealthy in burying an emerging government policy in an ad hoc report. Moynihan wrote a three-page outline for the redevelopment of Pennsylvania Avenue, which begins, "Pennsylvania Avenue should be the great thoroughfare of the city of Washington. Instead, it remains a vast, unformed, cluttered expanse at the heart of the nation's capital." Further, the report states, "Increasingly, the Capitol itself is cut off from the most developed part of the city by a blighted area that is unsightly by day and empty by night." The report concludes, "Pennsylvania Avenue should be lively, friendly, and inviting, as well as dignified and impressive."

Speaking about his role in Pennsylvania Avenue's redevelopment with a *Washington Post* reporter, Moynihan said that one could not call the area a slum, since "no one lived there." One would have assumed that a redevelopment proposal for Pennsylvania Avenue, attached to a report on alleviating a shortage in federal office space, would endorse—not criticize—the continuation of the efficient, impressive buildings of the Federal Triangle as an antidote to the misery of the north side of Pennsylvania Avenue. Instead, Moynihan's Trojan-horse proposal goes far beyond a simple recommendation for new office space, advocating a mixed-use plan of public and private buildings developed by public and private interests.

An immediate result of Moynihan's proposals was the formation of a President's Advisory Council on Pennsylvania Avenue, for which 11 members were named, including Moynihan. Nine of these were nationally prominent architects and landscape architects, and the chairman was Nathaniel Owings of Skidmore, Owings & Merrill.

Its unofficial status allowed the council to bypass normal government planning channels, such as the GSA. Working in their respective studios, the design professionals on the council produced voluminous work that included a large-scale model of the avenue, which Kennedy viewed in November 1963. Just before he left for Dallas, Kennedy dictated a memorandum directing that a coffee hour be scheduled for a group of invited senators to see the model and hear a formal presentation.

The devastation of Kennedy's assassination was alleviated somewhat by Lyndon Johnson's astute continuation of Kennedy's programs. The day after the funeral, Johnson asked Mrs. Kennedy which among her husband's works she most want carried out. She had two requests: rename Cape Canaveral after her husband in honor of his efforts on behalf of the space program and continue the Pennsylvania Avenue redevelopment effort. Johnson responded by accepting the formal report of the President's Advisory Council in April 1964. He thought well enough of the council's proposals to have them written into the 1964 Democratic Party platform.

Moynihan stayed on in the Johnson administration as assistant secretary of labor. He was there in March 1965 when Johnson reformed the council by executive order into the Temporary Commission on Pennsylvania Avenue. Owings returned as the chairman and Moynihan as vice chairman; and to many of the same returning architects from the unofficial council, the commission added the secretary of the Smithsonian Institution, the Architect of the Capitol, the director of the National Gallery of Art, several cabinet members, and other highly placed officials as members.

After a stint in academia in 1965 as a fellow at Wesleyan University's Center for Advanced Studies, and in 1966 as director of Harvard University's and the Massachusetts Institute of Technology's Joint Center for Urban Studies, Moynihan became an assistant for urban affairs to President Richard Nixon. He resumed his stewardship of the Pennsylvania Avenue redevelopment effort, then directly under his aegis. He had gained Nixon's support for the Temporary Commission on Pennsylvania Avenue as a condition of returning to Washington. That Nixon was a Republican—the leader of a party that at one level stands for government parsimony and limited public involvement—probably helped to champion a grand governmental project like the Pennsylvania Avenue redevelopment. Nixon personally lobbied Congress on behalf of a quasi-government development agency with vast powers of purchasing land and raising bond revenues. And with Moynihan, he took a walking tour of the avenue in September 1970. That day, Nixon sent a statement to Congress urging it to pass bills establishing a Federal City Bicentennial Development Corporation.

However, not until 1972 did Congress pass the enabling legislation to create the Pennsylvania Avenue Development Corporation (PADC). In the interim, Moynihan and Nixon were helped along by the self-evident fact that Pennsylvania Avenue had reached its absolute nadir. The April 1968 riots following Martin Luther King's assassination occurred farther uptown beyond Pennsylvania Avenue, but their consequences spread throughout the central business district. Shoppers fled to the suburban shopping malls that sprang up around the Beltway, and downtown businesses followed. Those that remained could ill afford to maintain their downtown investments, and many banks had redlined the avenue. Between 1960 and 1969, the Pennsylvania Avenue corridor suffered a 42 percent loss of business, and in 1969, there were ten completely vacant buildings in the corridor, and 82 more were vacant above the first floor.

Faced with this bleakness in its own front yard, Congress agreed that the 100-acre rectangular area surrounding Pennsylvania Avenue needed a blending of the federal presence with a variety of other community, residential, and commercial uses, very much in the vein that the White House—from the Kennedy, Johnson, and now the Nixon administrations—had been advocating. To accomplish this, PADC was given a broad range of powers, including the authority to sue and be sued in its own name, that is, without the protection of the U.S. government; to acquire property through eminent domain proceedings; to develop new and rehabilitated buildings; to manage property; to establish restrictions and standards ensuring conformance to the plan; to borrow money from the U.S. Treasury; to enforce the PADC plan with respect to construction of federal projects (typically exempt from local zoning and building codes, though not exempt from historic preservation regulations and overlays). PADC, as a federally owned agency, was exempt from local and federal taxes and property tax assessments, though Congress included in PADC's budget a setaside payment to the city in lieu of property taxes. In general, its powers were similar to those of city development entities, except that PADC held within it the powers of eminent domain and the power to regulate other agencies—two powers that are usually retained by the jurisdiction governing a development agency.

Of the 15-member board of directors, eight represented the private sector, and the remaining seven were high-level public officials, including four Cabinet members, the mayor of the District of Columbia, and the chairman of the city council. In addition, there were eight nonvoting members acting as liaisons to various organized arts, architecture, planning, and development interests in the city.

During the latter years of the Nixon administration, Moynihan was named a delegate to the United Nations and later was appointed ambassador to India, a post he held into the Gerald Ford administration, after which he served a year as permanent representative to the United Nations. By that time, his political views were sympathetic with those of neoconservatives, a newly forming influential group of 1960s liberals that had become disenchanted with big government. With their backing, Moynihan ran for and won the open seat as junior U.S. senator of New York in 1976, when he made his third and final trip to Washington—this time for four six-year terms.

Moynihan sought and gained membership on two significant Senate committees: environment and public works, and taxation. It was while on the former committee that Moynihan assumed statutory responsibilities for oversight of PADC affairs. M. Jay Brodie, PADC's executive director from 1984 to 1993, recalls that Moynihan exerted his influence by virtue of his widely known interest in Pennsylvania Avenue, historic preservation, and architecture in general and by virtue of his bipartisanship, having gathered his credentials from service in two Democratic and two Republican administrations and, more recently, having been elected as a Democratic senator with backing from neoconservatives. Brodie called on Moynihan's support on many occasions to advance PADC priorities, and he credits Moynihan's powers of persuasion combined with his perseverance with having prevented the Willard Hotel from being demolished, and with guiding the development of the International Center for Trade and Technology (now the Ronald Reagan Building and International Trade Center).

In the mid-1990s, after the completion of the last blocks on the north side of Pennsylvania Avenue, Congress declared the rehabilitation of Pennsylvania Avenue a success. In 1995, Congress moved to disband PADC on January 1, 1996. Fittingly,

Moynihan, who was there at the birth of PADC, was there to see its mission completed.

From his corner apartment in the Market Square condominiums, halfway between the Capitol and the White House, Moynihan can see the buildings of the two branches of government he served. His balcony overlooks the Navy Yard Memorial, which honors the veterans of the branch of the military in which he served as an officer and from which he retired as a reservist in 1966. He can see the Ronald Reagan Building, the capstone to his career as champion of PADC, and where, since his retirement from the Senate last year he has worked as a fellow at the Woodrow Wilson International Center for Scholars. He can in fact see every Pennsylvania Avenue building with which he has been involved.

Moynihan's condominium in Market Square is an urbanist's dwelling. Two centuries of monumental efforts of planning, designing, and building have made possible the boulevards and vistas. It is a fitting abode for the former secretary of housing and urban development, the former counselor to the president for urban affairs, the former Senate chairman for public works, and the articulator of America's urban condition. Moynihan would be the first to remind one that not he alone but many are responsible for PADC's legacy—developers risked money, planners planned, architects designed buildings, builders built, citizens advanced the common good with tax dollars. But it has taken visionaries—L'Enfant's successors—to advance America's Main Street from a planner's line on paper to the vibrant and grand allée that it is today. Daniel Patrick Moynihan's 40 years as champion of Pennsylvania Avenue and of the appropriateness of government interest in urban redevelopment is a unique contribution to America's development. ∎

2002

Retaining Value

Originally published in October 2002

Opposite: Diagonal Mar Centre, a 941,000-square-foot office building, completed in 2001, is the first phase of the 84-acre, $600 million, mixed-use waterfront community being developed in downtown Barcelona next to the Mediterranean Sea. *(Robert A.M. Stern)*

The philosophy of the Hines commercial real estate organization is straightforward: "Buildings of quality and architectural merit backed by responsive, professional management attract better tenants, command higher rents, and retain their value despite the ups and downs of the real estate market." Or, as Hines's founder and chairman Gerald D. Hines puts it, "For us, there was never a choice between building the mediocre or the magnificent. People expect high quality from us, and providing it has paid off." Now in its 45th year, Hines's Houston-based company is one of the world's largest, with properties around the globe valued at more than $13 billion and with offices in 76 U.S. cities and 11 countries overseas. The Hines name has become synonymous with high-quality construction and good practices—in architecture, building materials, sustainability, and business operations.

This dedication has earned Hines, 77, the 2002 ULI J.C. Nichols Prize for Visionaries in Urban Development, which recognizes civic-minded individuals employing innovative processes, techniques, and insights to obtain the highest-quality development practices and policies. The prize is named for legendary Kansas City, Missouri, developer Jesse Clyde Nichols, who was well known during the early 20th century for building cohesive, connected communities that instilled pride and a sense of permanence. J.C. Nichols died in 1950. Gerald Hines started developing buildings in the early 1950s, perhaps picking up where Nichols left off. Like Nichols, he insisted that his buildings be built not just for longevity, but to be appreciated. Like Nichols, he maintained that aesthetics and practical economics could be combined.

Hines is widely regarded as the visionary who raised the bar for commercial real estate development in the last half of the 20th century by commissioning top architects to design structures that would leave a distinctive imprint on the skyline. "Gerald Hines's greatest contribution is that he is a patron of architecture and, as a result, has made so much good work possible. He has shown, many times over, that design and quality do matter," says Joe Mashburn, dean of the Gerald D. Hines College of Architecture at the

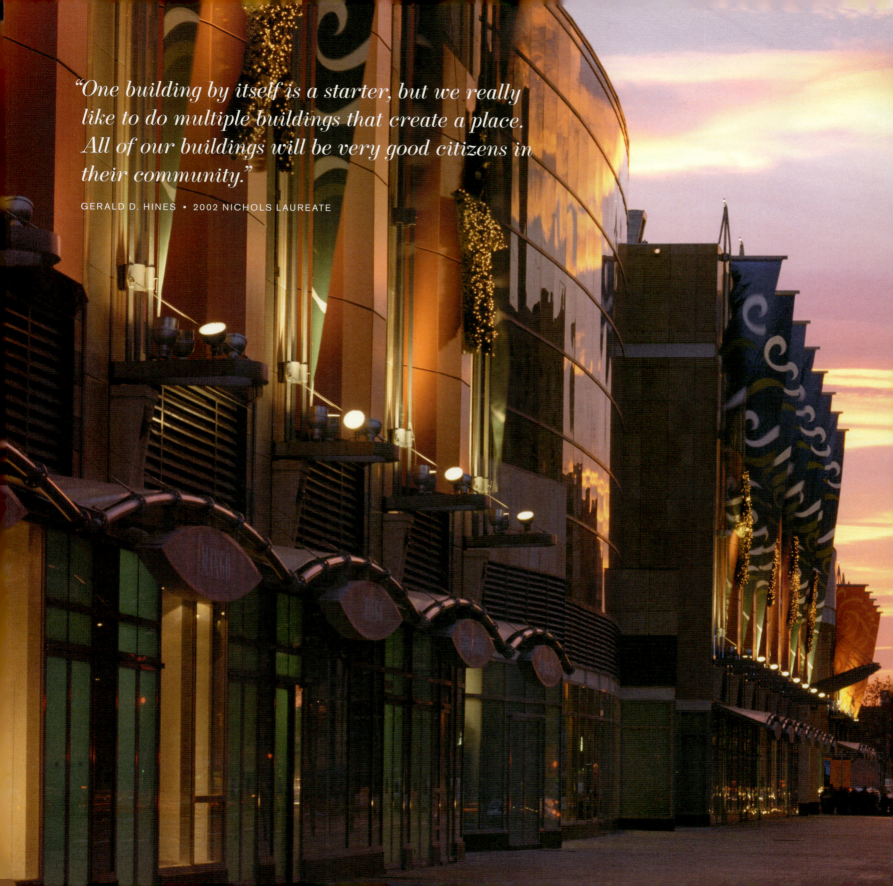

"One building by itself is a starter, but we really like to do multiple buildings that create a place. All of our buildings will be very good citizens in their community."

GERALD D. HINES • 2002 NICHOLS LAUREATE

University of Houston. "Hines is recognized as a giant of the industry among students of architecture. He has inspired a hopeful message that fostering good design can be a positive factor, not just for the development itself, but for the community as a whole."

Hines was selected to receive the Nichols Prize by a jury of five renowned urban experts: jury chair Robert C. Larson, chairman of Lazard Freres Real Estate Investors in New York City and chairman of the ULI Foundation; Paul Goldberger, architecture critic for *New Yorker* magazine; Peter S. Rummell, chairman and chief executive officer of the St. Joe Company in Jacksonville, Florida; Adele Chatfield-Taylor, president of the American Academy in Rome, with offices in New York City and Rome; and Joseph E. Brown, president and chief executive officer of EDAW Inc., in San Francisco.

A key aspect of the $100,000 prize, funded by an endowment from the J.C. Nichols family, is its use as a highly visible symbol of the importance of visionary community development, Larson explains. "Gerry Hines's personal integrity, his uncompromising commitment to quality, his use of world-class architects in the design of his properties, and his interest in environmental sustainability made him a compelling choice," says Larson.

"Gerry has a detailed view of the world, and good design comes from paying a lot of attention to details. It's something you spend a lot of hours poring over. Some people know how to do this. Others don't. Gerry does."

PETER S. RUMMELL • 2002 JURY MEMBER

By making architecture a marketable commodity, Hines "changed the nature of commercial real estate development more profoundly than anyone," notes Goldberger. "He pushed forward the frontiers of skyscraper design by showing that architecture and buildings put up to make money do not have to be incompatible. His charge to his architects has been 'Make an icon that people will remember and admire, not a building that will disappear into a bland background.' He uses architects who are site, place, and space specific, who will not just plop a shape they like anywhere but will do something that derives from the nature of the place."

Starting his career as a mechanical engineer, Hines built warehouses on the side for several years before founding Hines in 1957. His first skyscraper, the 50-story One Shell Plaza in Houston, designed by Skidmore, Owings & Merrill and completed in 1971, was the first of many subsequent projects to "give him knots in his stomach," he says with a chuckle. From the outset, Hines maintained that rather than sacrificing beauty for profit, beauty could be used to enhance it. "I was intrigued with trying to achieve quality architecture in office warehouses. We evolved a way to work with an architect and produce a building

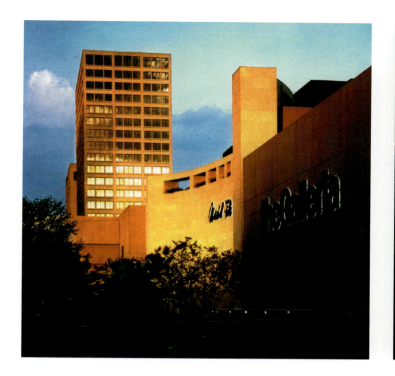

The 3 million-square-foot Houston Galleria, begun in 1967, includes 300 stores and restaurants, two hotels, three office towers, and an Olympic-size skating rink. *(Hellmuth, Obata + Kassabaum)*

in an economical way, and we got a lot of business because of our architecture," he says. "It used to be that if an architect worked for a developer, he was a second-class architect. But now, prominent architects are working with developers, and I think this has led to better cities and better places."

In addition to Skidmore, Owings & Merrill, other well-known architectural firms and architects who have designed for Hines include Kohn Pedersen Fox, Robert A.M. Stern Architects, Philip Johnson, Cesar Pelli, I.M. Pei, and Frank Gehry. "He was the first developer in modern times to incorporate quality architecture," says A. Eugene Kohn, president of Kohn Pedersen Fox Associates PC in New York City. "In the late 1940s, 1950s, and 1960s, a lot of development was less driven by quality and more driven by the bottom line. But Gerry Hines realized the value in designing buildings and workplaces that would make people proud—buildings they would want to show off."

Robert A.M. Stern attributes Hines's success to the ability to think long term, to spend what is necessary to produce a high-quality product that benefits not just the company, but the community as a whole. "Gerry Hines loves architecture, and he recognizes that through good design, you can enhance the revenue stream and create a building that gives something back to the community," Stern says.

Hines projects strive to combine beauty with functionality—many can be described as innovative, yet invitingly familiar and practical; daring, yet appropriate. "High-quality architecture does not mean that you throw away the budget. It means that you design the best product within that budget. You must adhere to certain disciplines or it [the project] is not a repeatable process," Hines says. "A repeatable process is one that is economically successful, not necessarily repeatable in the architecture, but in the process. We've done low-cost warehouses, but with a little flair, a little something extra. Not all our buildings are going to win an AIA [American Institute of Architects] award, but they will all be very good citizens in their community."

Two Hines projects—Houston's Pennzoil Place, developed in 1975, and Washington, D.C.'s Postal Square, renovated in 1992—have collectively won three of the AIA's highest awards for design. In fact, the company's projects have, as yet, received more than 140 awards, including three ULI Awards for Excellence: Comerica Tower at Detroit Center, 1996; Wells Fargo Center in Minneapolis, 1989; and the Galleria in Houston, 1979.

"In the beginning, architects were receptive but skeptical about working with us since developers had raped the landscape for so many years," says Hines. "When I look back, I am most proud of the innovation we initiated in some of those landmark projects, such as Pennzoil Place and the Houston Galleria. Those were big mountains to climb, and with the net worth we had at the time, we were probably overreaching," he adds. Over the years, the company's work has expanded to virtually all real estate product categories:

SINCE RECEIVING THE NICHOLS PRIZE IN 2002

Gerald Hines, center, congratulates the winning team members from the University of Maryland for their proposal to transform Nashville's Sulphur Dell in the 2014 Student Urban Design Competition. *(Nathan Weber)*

Gerald D. Hines has continued his decades-long commitment to creating projects of the highest quality, aesthetic relevance, and enduring value for partners, clients, and communities, as well as for his firm's investor partners and clients.

During this time, the company has grown from $13 billion to over $28 billion of global assets under management. With a presence in more than 115 cities around the globe, Hines remains one of the largest real estate organizations in the world. The Hines portfolio of projects underway, completed, acquired, or managed for third parties consists of more than 1,300 properties, including skyscrapers, corporate headquarters, mixed-use centers, industrial parks, medical facilities, and master-planned resort and residential communities.

A firm believer in the power of people and fostering transformative values, Hines declined the Nichols prize money and matched it with an additional $100,000 to seed the annual ULI Gerald D. Hines Student Urban Design Competition. The

office, industrial, retail, residential, mixed-use, and master-planned communities. In addition to the trapezoidal Pennzoil Place and the shopping/office/hotel Galleria complex in Houston, some of the more well-known U.S. projects include the cylindrical 101 California Street in San Francisco; Franklin Square, near the White House; and the "Lipstick Building" at 53rd Street and Third Avenue in Manhattan.

Much of Hines's overseas work, particularly in Europe, has required the ability to cope with much tougher land use restrictions and adapt to cultural differences. "It's a Herculean task," Hines says. "One of our biggest challenges is building communities in different countries with different cultures and figuring out how we can adapt to each. In each one, there is a certain level of acceptance of what they perceive as a quality project." Two European projects currently rank among the company's largest: in Munich, Hines is building several towers, including a 38-floor building with 950,000 square feet; in Paris, it is developing a 10 million-square-foot project on the former Renault factory site.

Nichols Prize jury member Chatfield-Taylor, a historic preservationist, points out that Hines has the foresight to ensure that his buildings enhance and reinforce the tradition, history, and character of their surroundings—which can be a challenge in older European cities. "To incorporate new pieces into delicate cities while advancing historic preservation, to prove that you can make an addition to historic cities without ruining them, is marvelously

A 48-story, 1.2 million-square-foot cylindrical office tower located in the heart of San Francisco's financial district, 101 California Street was completed in 1982. *(Johnson/Burgee Associates)*

ideas competition challenges multidisciplinary teams of graduate students from universities in the United States and Canada to offer practical, workable solutions to an urban development problem identified in an actual site in a major urban area. Since founding the competition, Hines endowed the program with a $3 million gift.

The competition has become a pivotal experience for graduate students as they prepare for careers in the built environment. Since the competition began in 2003, more than 6,200 students on nearly 1,200 teams have participated. "The purpose of the competition is to raise awareness, particularly among the next generation, of the important role that high-quality urban design plays in creating not just beautiful buildings, but living environments," Hines says. The competition encourages cooperation and teamwork among future real estate developers and the many allied professions such as architecture, landscape architecture, historic preservation, engineering, finance, and others.

To be more involved with students, Hines served in 2005 as the inaugural fellow for the Edward P. Bass Distinguished Visiting Architecture Fellowship at the Yale School of Architecture. The program brings developers together with senior design students to review an active development in the fellow's firm.

Hines's legacy of making contributions to urban areas that withstand the test of time continues to set a course of excellence for future generations of community builders. "Gerry is a visionary in every sense of the word," says Richard M. Rosan, former ULI president. "Through his personal integrity, his uncompromising commitment to high quality, his pursuit of environmental sustainability, and his desire to give back to his profession and to communities in general, Gerry has created a success formula few can emulate. He has shown many times over that design and quality do matter, and our global built environment is all the better for it." ■

The 34-story, 592,000-square-foot office tower 53rd at Third, completed in Manhattan in 1986, was dubbed the "Lipstick Building" by its architect, Philip Johnson, for its elongated elliptical volume and its red granite banding. (Johnson/Burgee Associates)

invigorating," she says. "So often, people dread the arrival of a new building, but when it is a positive experience, the whole attitude of a community can be changed. . . . The buildings that are being built today will be the preservation issues of the future. And there will be some additions to the built world that will be easier to love later on—100, 200 years from now—than others."

One of Hines's newer projects, and one of which Gerald Hines is particularly proud, is Diagonal Mar in Barcelona, Spain. Located downtown on 84 acres next to the Mediterranean Sea, the $600 million, mixed-use community, being developed in phases, will cover 4 million square feet including a regional retail and leisure center, 1,400 apartments, three hotels, three office buildings, and a 540,000-square-foot convention facility, all surrounded by a 35-acre public park, the city's third largest. Diagonal Mar was chosen last year as the "most innovative real estate project in Barcelona" by the Premios Imobiliarios Quatrium organization. "It's a great urban project, probably the most diverse community we've developed, and I believe it will be known worldwide," says Hines.

Developing Diagonal Mar was hardly easy; for example, to prevent water infiltration, Hines had to build a half-mile-long wall 200 feet below grade to keep the sea from seeping into the underground parking garage and undermining the facility. "It was certainly complicated," comments Stern, the design architect for the project. But it is Hines's nature to "roll up his sleeves" and find solutions to obstacles, Stern says, noting that Gerry Hines does not shy away from tackling complex, controversial projects. Kohn of Kohn Pedersen Fox points out that because Hines is willing to take risks and "try something different," he encourages architects to be daring and innovative. "Gerry does not surround himself with 'yes' people. He wants other opinions, he listens to his team and to his architects, and he is always ready to learn something new," Kohn says.

Hines's background as an engineer instilled in him a penchant for details, which has contributed to the success of his buildings, notes Nichols Prize jurist Rummell. "Gerry has a detailed view of the world, as well as a global view, and good design comes from paying a lot of attention to details. You have to start with a vision that goes beyond what you are working on, but then you have to execute against that vision, and the execution is in the details," points out Rummell. "That's not something you phone in. It's something you spend a lot of hours poring over and putting yourself in the consumer's position of how that project will be experienced. Some people know how to do this. Others don't. Gerry does."

Over the years, the Hines firm has concentrated more on developing mixed-use projects combining residential and commercial uses than on developing single signature towers. "One building by itself is a starter, but we really like to do multiple buildings that create a place," Hines says. "Well-planned urban design must include innovative programs so it's not just retail and office space. You must have other elements—such as housing, recreation, entertainment—that interact to create a quality background."

Like many other longtime real estate industry experts, Hines has seen urban growth patterns in the United States deteriorate throughout much of his career, with many people stuck in traffic as they make their way through haphazard, poorly connected development— a stark contrast to many European communities, which emphasize tightly linked, pedestrian-

A Really Energetic Guy

Two years ago, to celebrate turning 75, fitness enthusiast Gerald D. Hines donned his in-line skates and took off up a mountain outside of Aspen, where he owns a vacation home and spends part of each year. There are far flatter pedestrian trails that weave throughout the town—certainly enough of them for a thorough workout. But sticking to those would have been too easy. Hines does not like to do just enough—he prefers to excel and challenge himself in the process. And that is the approach he has used in building the Hines firm from a single-room, office warehouse construction company in 1957 into a multibillion-dollar, multifaceted real estate organization with offices worldwide.

According to Hines, this year's winner of the Nichols Prize, part of his company's success is based on the ability to be both a local company and international company, serving specific market needs in many corners of the world. Although Hines's central offices remain in Houston, the firm has seven regional divisions, including four that cover foreign markets; within each region are multiple offices. "One of the strengths of our organization is our regional capability, in which we act as a local developer, yet we are an international developer," Hines says. The regional structure, which was somewhat unusual in the industry when Hines initiated it years ago, is a "constantly evolving" operation involving shifts in authority between the headquarters and regional offices, he explains.

Hines's son, Jeff, 47, joined the firm in 1981 and became president in 1990. "Dad did a very good job of creating the organization with an entrepreneurial feel that is necessary to operate in real estate at the local level. Yet, at the same time, it has the benefits of scale, of having an international reputation, of having financial clout, and of being in a position to allocate capital. All of those aspects are important to succeed in the strategy we've chosen," he notes. "Decisions that are market specific, such as deciding what constitutes a good site or a bad site, have to be made by the regional people. But in terms of managing the capital of the firm or its reputation, there must be policies with a central focus."

For example, the company's longtime policy of conservative development financing applies to all its projects, throughout economic booms as well as busts. This tendency to take on minimal debt has served it well, allowing it to remain healthy and expand during the 1980s, when many real estate companies folded. "We've had a lot of economic bumps, and what we've tried to do is maintain a higher percentage of equity, not as much debt, and build the best building in the marketplace at the time," Gerald Hines says. Currently, the company is using more institutional funds to finance several project in different markets, rather than relying on local financing sources for individual projects, Jeff Hines says. "This creates more glue between the regions and it adds another player to the process, the fund manager, who is by definition a central person. This provides a bit of balance to the whole structure."

The firm is privately held: it is owned by Gerald and Jeff Hines. However, Hines's senior management participates in the profits and losses. With an average tenure of more than 25 years, the executive team members have a well-established stake in the company's course. "Everyone is given a fair degree of freedom, and compensation is based on individual performance. There is a strong feeling of entrepreneurialism that has been here since day one," Jeff Hines observes. "We have a philosophy of hiring really top-notch people early in their careers who tend to make a lifetime career at Hines. People here have grown up working with the same group of people, so it [the company] has a collegial feel. We focus on promoting from within, on providing meaningful career paths, and this culture is an important part of what Dad did to make the company successful." Instilling a strong sense of integrity has proved critical in the firm's overseas expansion, he notes. "As we get more far-flung in terms of operations, it's important that our people in those regions are making decisions within a construct that is consistent with how we would act if we [the central office] were there."

Gerald Hines, who lives in London, now spends much of his time overseeing the company's European operations, while his son runs Hines's U.S. headquarters and oversees activities in Asia and Latin America. For the elder Hines, releasing day-to-day control of the entire operation was made easier by the experience and loyalty of the company's top management. "The most important aspect of building this company has been to get good leaders and let them participate. They are with us for the long term, not as a job-hopping opportunity," he says.

As the years have passed, being able to trust others with the company has allowed Hines free time to pursue his personal interests: skating, skiing, cycling, tennis, and enjoying his family. "You always regret that you did not spend more time with your family. But I think I've maintained a reasonable balance between work and family, and I look forward to many years of being with my family," he says.

Jeff Hines is quick to clarify that while he relishes time with his father, he's not likely to join him in any future skiing expedition at the peaks of Aspen. "I think most people would definitely strive to be in the shape he's in at 77," he says with a smile. "Dad is a unique individual, a really energetic guy." ∎

friendly development. Hines and his company support denser projects along transit lines, and Hines notes he is encouraged by the transit-oriented development occurring in communities throughout the nation.

While Hines stops short of calling denser development a large-scale trend in the United States, he believes that the desire of Americans to sacrifice convenience for size may be fading—at least some. "As cities get more congested and people have less discretionary time, I think we'll see more people choosing smaller spaces in central cities, and we'll see more developers making them [closer-in locations and central cities] better places to live," he says. "Urban areas need smaller units and higher density with transit alternatives or they will strangle," maintains Hines. "The quality of infrastructure in Europe is so much greater than what we have in the United States, and the inner-city development that has not happened here is because of the lack of transit. Our transportation technology will evolve, but it will be much more expensive to go back and develop it, than to have it in place originally. We will have dense cores because people will demand them. They'll pay a higher price per square foot to increase their discretionary time," he adds.

In addition to density, Hines is interested in the continued development of environmentally conscious, green buildings. Since 1992, his company has been a partner in the U.S. Environmental Protection Agency's (EPA) Energy Star program, which recognizes projects meeting EPA standards for superior energy management and conservation. Hines projects have received more than 50 Energy Star Label awards, and the company was named Energy Star Partner of the year in 2001 and 2002. "Our tenants are seeking more energy-efficient buildings. That is a trend our culture is moving toward, and we want to be the most proficient in that area that we can be. It will be a competitive issue, and we want to continue to differentiate ourselves," Hines says.

Hines's desire to contribute to a better urban environment—not just produce a better building—exemplifies the ideals of the Nichols Prize, explains jury member Brown. "The prize is about the full composition of community, not just about building the best building in the world. Gerry Hines has moved beyond signature buildings to a level of concern with infrastructure, with parks and the public realm, and with integrating sustainability principles into his work," Brown says. "It's a remarkable evolution from high-quality architecture and design to community. Gerry builds communities with a sense that they will be here forever. He's never doing it for the short run."

Opposite: Originally built as Norwest Tower in 1988, the Wells Fargo Center is a stepped, 57-story, 1.1 million-square-foot headquarters building located in downtown Minneapolis. *(Cesar Pelli & Associates)*

2003

The Architecture of Community

Originally published in October 2003

(Catherine Lynn)

Opposite: Duany Plater-Zyberk & Company: Seaside (1990s). First a laboratory and later a model for the new urbanism, Seaside was planned by two students of Scully, who among many others have applied the lessons of Scully's teachings to their practices as architects and planners. *(Steven Brooke)*

Vincent Scully, one of the nation's foremost architectural historians, as well as a longtime Yale University professor, has been selected as the fourth annual laureate of the ULI J.C. Nichols Prize for Visionaries in Urban Development. Scully, 83, who has taught several generations of architects, planners, art historians, developers, and politicians throughout his distinguished career, has been described by renowned architect Philip Johnson as "the most influential architecture teacher, ever."

The Nichols Prize recognizes a person whose career demonstrates a commitment to the highest standards of responsible development. The $100,000 prize honors the legacy of legendary Kansas City, Missouri, developer J.C. Nichols, a founding ULI member and considered one of America's most influential entrepreneurs in land use during the first half of the 1900s.

Scully was selected to receive the Nichols Prize by a jury of five distinguished urban experts: jury chair Peter S. Rummell, chairman and chief executive officer of the St. Joe Company in Jacksonville, Florida; Paul Goldberger, architecture critic for the *New Yorker* magazine; Adele Chatfield-Taylor, president of the American Academy in Rome; Joseph E. Brown, president and chief executive officer of EDAW Inc., in San Francisco; and James A. Ratner, executive vice president of Forest City Enterprises in Cleveland.

As the fourth recipient of the Nichols Prize, Scully follows two public officials—Charleston, South Carolina, Mayor Joseph P. Riley Jr. and the late U.S. Senator Daniel Patrick Moynihan—and a private sector representative, Gerald D. Hines, founder and chairman of the Hines real estate organization. Riley, Moynihan, and Hines were the 2000, 2001, and 2002 Nichols Prize laureates, respectively.

The selection of Scully—an academic—represents an additional aspect of the built environment that is recognized by the Nichols Prize, Rummell notes. "It takes academics to create an intellectual stimulus, which is what the award was designed to celebrate," Rummell says. "Nobody has thought about the community design in a richer way than Vincent Scully. The people he has taught have had enormous influence on urban planning and design . . . they understand that architecture is but one piece of what you do, and

"*The city is precious to us. But no one of us is capable of understanding all the multiple forces that shape it. Architects and developers now perceive that their work together involves the human city entire. The whole manmade environment in relation to the natural world is our proper study now, and that is a cooperative effort. Alone, one can hardly grasp it all.*"

VINCENT SCULLY · 2003 NICHOLS LAUREATE

W.G. Low House (1887), Bristol, Rhode Island. For his first book—on the significance of such domestic architecture as the iconic Low House—Vincent Scully coined the term "shingle style," now a staple of the architectural lexicon. *(McKim, Mead, and White)*

that only when planning is done in the whole that a sense of place is achieved. Scully has a great ability to put things in context, to show that urban design is not just about architecture."

Scully's selection as 2003 Nichols Prize laureate is a tribute to "using the power of ideas to influence development," says Goldberger, who studied under Scully. "His thinking has always been based on the notion that architecture is not purely aesthetics and that [its] real meaning is how it can be used to make better places. He had taught the social value of architecture not just to architects, but to lawyers, real estate developers, and others who have made the world a better place."

According to Ratner, Scully's teachings have reached far beyond his students. "As developers, we are building communities, and we know that an individual building does not make the community. Vincent Scully has emphasized this, and [as a result] he has directly influenced and touched development and architecture," Ratner says. "He is sensitive to context, what development patterns are, and that the success of development depends on having livable communities. Without question, our communities would look different without him, because the people he has influenced have, over time, influenced the built environment."

For more than 55 years, Vincent Scully has been teaching introductory courses and advanced seminars—mostly at Yale University, and since 1991, at the University of Miami—that inspire and inform and, above all, help form the intellectual underpinnings of many successful careers. He is the rare historian who has made a name for himself by his interpretation of history and his shaping of history. His lectures, writings, and mentoring have influenced the course of modern urban development and fueled the burgeoning new urbanism movement.

Scully graduated from Yale University in 1940 with a major in English literature and enrolled in graduate school in the English department. Disenchanted with the department's preoccupation with the New Criticism, he joined the military and served in both the Mediterranean and Pacific theaters of World War II. He returned to Yale in 1946 as a graduate student in the art history department and earned a doctorate in 1949 with a dissertation on 19th-century American domestic architecture. In 1947, he was hired as a lecturer in art history at Yale, where he has taught for the past 56 years. His teaching abilities and his understanding of the subject became legendary and his classes were much sought after (see feature box, "On Vincent Scully as the Big Bang"). But he was equally distinguished in his research and publications. Beginning with the publication in 1955 of his doctoral dissertation as a book, *The Shingle Style: Architectural Theory and Design from Richardson to the Origins of Wright,* Scully was well on his way to defining architecture as a "continuing dialogue between generations that creates an environment across time" and changing the way scholars and practitioners viewed many aspects of architecture and architectural history.

Choosing architecture as the subject of his art history PhD dissertation signaled Scully's move toward the built environment. Even as a child, Scully had imagined what the floor plans of the houses must be like as he walked past them in the native New Haven,

Connecticut, residential neighborhood; there and in nearby Rhode Island were houses he could visit, analyze, and understand. He was particularly taken with the Low House, designed by McKim, Mead, and White in 1887, and with what he called "The Stick and Shingle Style" cottages of Newport, Scully saw in American vernacular architecture, culminating in the early work of Frank Lloyd Wright, an indigenous creativity that explored and exploited spatial forms.

Scully was among the first to recognize that Wright was a unique genius who nevertheless grew directly out of the American vernacular traditions, leading to a rich modern architecture and influencing the work of the early masters of the International Style—Walter Gropius and Mies van der Rohe to Le Corbusier. As his appreciation for those architects of the heroic period matured, however, Scully began to see in their ideological positions—although not necessarily in their architecture—implications that ran counter to his own understanding of the urban context. He became critical of Wright's tendency to run away from the city, extolling suburbanism without understanding the implications of unfettered suburban sprawl. Scully saw Wright's fascination with automobiles as dangerous for the urban future.

In 1951, Scully traveled to Italy on a Fulbright scholarship to study the art and architecture of Italy and Greek colonial architecture in Italy. While visiting ancient and medieval sites, he was struck by how the ancients placed their temples in their environments yet how classical archaeologists generally ignored the landscape settings of their buildings. Scully looked beyond the mute ruins and focused on the surrounding landscape. If the

Le Corbusier: Contemporary City. Scully acknowledged the form makers of the heroic period in modern architecture, such as Le Corbusier, but criticized the architect's planning proposal for a "city for 3 million inhabitants," which happily was not executed.

Frank Lloyd Wright, Robie House (1910), Chicago, Illinois. While crediting Wright with advancing American vernacular architecture as a precursor to the International Style, Scully recognized that Wright's idealized view of a suburban nation was dangerous for the future of cities. *(Courtesy of the Frank Lloyd Wright Preservation Trust/ Hedrich Blessing)*

On Vincent Scully as the Big Bang

In honoring Vincent Scully as the 2003 laureate of the ULI J.C. Nichols Prize for Visionaries in Urban Development, jury members cited his continuing contribution as a teacher of generations of architects and consumers of architecture since he first stepped to the lecturer's podium at Yale University in 1947. His views are far reaching as his students became teachers and practitioners, and those who did not used his teachings consciously and subconsciously throughout their lives, whatever their professions. Those students who remained in the design professions kept in touch with their mentor. This iterative and evolving feedback informed every successive generation of students, just as it informed Scully, who altered and refined his own views over the years. By this ripple effect among practitioners and nonpractitioners, Scully has done as much to influence "visionary urban development" as those who are involved with actual sticks and stones.

Scully was recognized as a uniquely influential teacher as early as 1966 by *Time* magazine, in an article, "Great Teachers," and by *People* magazine in 1975, in "12 Great U.S. Professors." In 1976, the American Institute of Architects accorded him an honorary membership and an award for his teaching. His last Yale lecture to his history of modern architecture students in 1991—when Yale's mandatory retirement policy made him an emeritus professor— was covered as a front-page article in the *New York Times*.

So what are his classes like?

His survey course, "Introduction to the History of Art," is among the most popular classes at Yale; the law school's 500-seat auditorium is one of the few campus venues that can accommodate it. Students, many of them auditing the course, and visitors take up most of the seats; more stand along the side walls and at the back. Scully strides in, and with few introductory remarks, the lights go down, and the slide projector image illuminates the screen. He lectures without notes as each slide cues an outpouring of lyrical and passionate observation and analyses. Carrying an eight-foot pole, he uses it as a pointer, a paintbrush, a cudgel. He may jab at

Scully holding forth in 1959. *(Robert A.M. Stern Architects)*

the screen, sending the projected image into shivers. At the hour's end, even a casual visitor knows that this was a lecture unlike another, and all applaud as the lights come back up.

A February 18, 1980, *New Yorker* magazine profile retells a student's anecdote: "At the beginning of his first class, Scully stands up there in front of the screen and says, 'Turn off the lights.' The lights go off, and all the weenies in the class are immediately thrown into panic. They can't see to take notes. How are they going to get their A? The next time the class meets they all bring flashlight pens. When Scully turns off the lights, the hall looks as if it were full of lightning bugs. Scully tells them to put away the pens—there will be no note taking allowed in his course. 'You're distracting those who want to learn,' he says."

The same article quotes Robert F. Thompson, a fellow art history professor at Yale, ". . . a lot of his students have caught fire from his sun, taken some of that solar gaseous stuff and spun their own galaxies." Here are what some of those "stars" say about the *deus ex machina* of their solar systems.

Scully as a teacher

PAUL GOLDBERGER, architecture critic (*New Yorker* magazine): We have always all been his students because we never stopped being his students. Architects, scholars, critics, city planners, preservationists, urbanites, and those who pass through his class who never connected directly to these fields—because of Vince, they become better clients, more civilized bankers, maybe more honorable politicians.

DANIEL ROSE, developer (Rose Associates Inc., New York): I was a student in the late '40s, at the beginning of Vince's career. He stopped right in the middle of a lecture, turned to face the class, and he said, "I think what I just said was gibberish. It looked good when I thought of it last night, but it's gibberish." Who else would do that?

DAVID McCULLOUGH, writer and historian (*Truman, John Adams, The Path Between the Seas, Mornings on Horseback*): Once I told Professor Scully about a book that I had just read and that I liked very much and later he told me that he had gone and bought a copy and read it too. Never had a teacher paid me such a compliment.

Scully as an insipirer

ELIZABETH PLATER-ZYBERK, architect (Duany Plater-Zyberk & Company, Miami) and dean (University of Miami): Many of us left Yale determined to carry on in our practices the traditions of American architecture which he taught us—so gloriously espoused in his lectures—an influence more powerful than any design studio critique.

ROBERT A.M. STERN, architect (Robert A.M. Stern and Associates, New York), and dean (Yale University): Scully has taught us that we need not be embarrassed to be American architects. He has helped us to appreciate our American culture as something more than a footnote to European experience, as something distinct with its own dignity and even grandeur.

DAVID CHILDS, architect (Skidmore, Owings & Merrill, New York): Thirty years ago a sophomore pre-med student went to a 53b lecture. One hour later he decided to switch to a major in architecture. I was that sophomore pre-med student.

Scully as an urbanist

JONATHAN BARNETT, professor (University of Pennsylvania): Vincent Scully put architecture in context for us, as part of cities and as part of human history.

STERN: He has never wavered in his belief that the great purpose of architecture is not to build monuments but to build communities.

Scully as a visionary

CON HOWE, planner (director of planning, City of Los Angeles): Before there was the new urbanism, there was Vincent Scully.

ANDRÉS DUANY, architect (Duany Plater-Zyberk & Company, Miami): Vincent Scully has time and again been prescient. Twenty-five years ago he saw that the sprawling living pattern of the American middle class was the root cause of our dismal social and ecological situation. He taught us how for 300 years we had made much better places to live.

Scully continues his full-time teaching career with a fall semester class at Yale and a spring semester class as Distinguished Visiting Professor at the University of Miami. His wife, Catherine Lynn, is also on the visiting faculties at Yale and Miami, and they live in Lynchburg, Virginia, during summers.

Thanks to the National Building Museum for providing many of the quotations from Vincent Scully's students. ∎

The Acropolis in Athens, Greece, and Taos Pueblo in Taos, New Mexico. With his studies of Greek temples and Native American pueblos, Scully began his move in emphasis from the building as object to the building in context. *(Corbis)*

classical approach was deductive, Scully's was inductive. He wrote in *The Earth, the Temple, and the Gods: Greek Sacred Architecture* (1962)—the book that arose from years of research at those sites—"The landscape and the temples together form the architectural whole . . . and must therefore be seen in relation to each other." This approach—the move in emphasis from the object to the context—was initially rejected by mainstream archaeologists, but today is accepted as normative.

Scully found a new way to advance his argument in the summer of 1964 when he visited the American Southwest. There, in the precolonial architecture of New Mexico, Scully saw the antithesis to the Greek's contrast between architecture and landscape: he saw accommodation, not confrontation. While the ancient Greeks built their temples with columns that contrasted with the landscape and stressed the human character of their divinity, Native Americans built their temples to mimic the landscape with pyramidal forms that echoed those of their sacred mountains. His research and scholarship resulted in *Pueblo: Mountain, Village, Dance* (1975). These two opposing theses—confrontation in *The Earth, the Temple, and the Gods* and accommodation in *Pueblo*—and his studies on French Renaissance gardens, reached a grand summation in *Architecture: The Natural and the Manmade* (1991). The book synopsized Scully's works of scholarship and established a stepping-stone to an increasing concern for the power of architecture to build community and civility and its dark corollary: the ways in which bad design can destroy a community or the life of a city.

Injustice, however small, is a constant that Scully has always confronted. He still winces in recalling his anguish at an early age when he first heard the Welsh story of Gêlert, the faithful dog, who was killed by his master who suspected the dog of foul play, when in fact, Gêlert had heroically saved the life of his charge, the master's child. Another lesson learned in childhood was brought home to Scully in the fourth grade, when the young Scully challenged his teacher—who had asserted that tigers were native to Africa—with a citation from *Compton's Encyclopedia*, which the teacher refused to accept.

Closer to home, Scully became an activist in New Haven, whose urban redevelopment efforts he introduced as an illustrative example of contemporary urbanism gone awry in *American Architecture and Urbanism* (1969). He decried the obliteration of much of New Haven's low-income housing stock to make way for the Oak Street Connector, which was planned to route commuters quickly in and out of the city. He fought to curtail further redevelopment efforts around New Haven's central green, which threatened to destroy historic buildings.

Scully's confrontations with injustice also are tied to his antiheroic stance, previously seen in his defense of housing for the poor and in his critiques of modern architecture by megalomaniacal architects. This is not to say that he is against bold or courageous thought and action—quite the contrary, he has written persuasively about heroic architects, public officials, and ambitious projects. Whereas his academic subject matter was necessarily tied to "heroic" architects and their architecture, and "heroic" concepts of man in nature, Scully has chosen antiheroic positions throughout his career.

His antiheroism comes to a focus in *The Shingle Style Today, or, the Historian's Revenge* (1974), the title of which suggests a sequel to his landmark book on the shingle style. Here, Scully exacts his "historians revenge" by pointing out that modern architecture continues to refuse to acknowledge the influence of history, while relevant architecture being practiced by such architects as Robert Venturi was "critically influenced" by history and was a part of the mainstream that reflected American aspirations.

> *"Vincent Scully's thinking has always been based on the notion that architecture is not purely aesthetics, and that its real meaning is how it can be used to make better places."*
>
> PAUL GOLDBERGER • 2003 JURY MEMBER

In "The Death of the Street" and "Doldrums in the Suburbs," two articles from the mid-1960s, Scully pioneered what has come to be called contextualism. He dissected the new buildings on Park Avenue—focusing primarily on Lever House—and points out that they "cut a hole in the wall that defined the Avenue." Their *raisons d'être* not only "owed everything to the preexisting civility of the street," but also the new buildings were "taking a step toward its destruction." Scully called for leadership to "discipline anarchy in order to make the city what it has always been, the ultimate work of human art: making possible the effective action not only of the group but of the individual citizen." He called for a "return to the vernacular and classical traditions and their reintegration into the mainstream of modern architecture in its [most] fundamental aspect: the structure of Communities, the building of towns." Only by creating a secure and habitable place for the group can there be freedom for the individual, Scully maintained.

Robert Venturi: Guild House (1963), Philadelphia, Pennsylvania. With his defense of the Guild House and his introductory essay to Robert Venturi's *Complexity and Contradiction in Architecture* (1966), Scully established himself as Venturi's first and principal champion. *(William Watkins)*

Such concerns are again evident in Scully's championing of the new urbanism, especially as practiced by Andrés Duany and Elizabeth Plater-Zyberk, his students from the early 1970s. Their adoption of planning and design codes to discipline "egotistical" architects gives communities the chance to evolve physically while pursuing certain social objectives that benefit the entire community. Buildings that honor and respect their neighbors encourage democratic initiatives and a balance in society. Codes foster a communal sense, encouraging citizens to become communally responsible. Scully wrote, "Architecture is fundamentally a matter not of individual buildings but of the shaping of community, and that . . . is done by the law." Scully points out that codes promote the role architecture and design play in creating a strong sense of place, which he refers to as the "architecture of community." He described this movement in a foreword he wrote in 2000 for ULI's publication *Density by Design*. "Americans today seem to feel that a sense of community is exactly what needs to be revived in this country, and many apparently want exactly that for themselves and their families. It is therefore no great wonder that they are choosing to live in the kind of integrated architectural groupings that are suggestive of the towns in which they grew up, or about which they have always dreamed."

SINCE RECEIVING THE NICHOLS PRIZE IN 2003

Vincent Scully has continued his legacy as one of the most influential architectural scholars in the nation. From his lectures at Yale University and the University of Miami to his written works such as *American Architecture and Urbanism* and *The Earth, the Temple, and the Gods: Greek Sacred Architecture*, Scully has made a lasting impression on the American development culture. Though Scully is no longer found at the front of a large lecture hall since retiring in 2008, his thoughts and influence can still be seen through the research and works he continued to produce. In 2004, Scully cowrote the book *Yale in New Haven: Architecture and Urbanism*, which includes an incisive overview of the architectural relationship between Yale and New Haven, Connecticut.

Scully has also received many awards from other organizations in recognition of his important contributions to the arts and architecture. In 2004, President George W. Bush presented Scully with the National Medal of Arts, the country's highest honor for artists and arts patrons. The medal citation reads: "For his remarkable contributions to the history of design

and modern architecture, including his influential teaching as an architectural historian." In 2010, Scully received the Louise du Pont Cornwinshield Award from the National Trust for Historic Preservation, received the Henry Hope Reed Award from Notre Dame, and was named a fellow of the Society of Architectural Historians.

In 2010, the Checkerboard Film Foundation, known for creating films about individuals who make unique and important contributions to the American arts, produced its documentary *Vincent Scully: An Art Historian among Architects*. It features important moments in Scully's life as a teacher and mentor, with past students telling how Scully changed their lives and work. "Terrible subject but nice movie," Scully said of the documentary in an interview with the *Yale Daily News*. Aside from these projects and accolades, Scully is taking advantage of his retirement and spending time with his wife, Catherine Lynn, in Lynchburg, Virginia. ■

The Oak Street Connector—a roadway intended to route commuters quickly in and out of downtown New Haven—is Scully's hometown example of urban development gone awry. *(Greg Amy)*

The balance between freedom and order, or the individual and the law, and the institutionalization of the battle against injustice has been a common thread throughout Scully's writings about urbanism. He cites Ambrogio Lorenzetti's fresco, *Allegory of Good Government*, which he saw as a Fulbright scholar. In it, he sees all the characteristics of the well-planned, that is, livable, city: a city dense with activity, but peaceful and secure. In the allegory, the citizens voluntarily grasp a golden cord, symbolic of the law that binds them and makes them free. For Scully, this allegory symbolizes "architecture that is made possible by good government—decent policy, the consent of the governed, justice, and peace."

In the final analysis, historians—even Scully—do not shape history so much as inform the next generation that creates history. Furthermore, the stock in trade for historians is the retelling of the past, not the foretelling of the future. But Scully, historian of man and culture, has shaped a most important aspect of American real estate development—human habitation—and in hindsight, he has foretold the future in which we now live.

Scully is rooted in New Haven and in Yale University. He was born there, earned his degrees there, teaches there, has spent his entire life there, and recently wrote a history of New Haven and the Yale campus. His legacy at Yale University will be ensured through the chaired professorship that Yale established in his name in 1997 and the recent (anonymous) endowment of the Vincent I. Scully Jr. Visiting Professorship in Architectural History. Despite Scully's lifelong tenure in the art history department, this second chair is housed in the school of architecture—a fitting and happy climax in the anomalous career of the 2003 laureate of the ULI J.C. Nichols Prize for Visionaries in Urban Development.

2004

Urban Pioneer

Originally published in October 2004

(MBS)

Opposite: McCormack Baron Salazar's Harmony Oaks community in Central City New Orleans is recognized as a cutting-edge, exceptional affordable housing development. *(MBS)*

To a visitor driving through the Murphy Park neighborhood in St. Louis on a perfect summer day with moderate temperatures and low humidity, the signs of community pride are evident: well-landscaped lawns are filled with maturing trees and shrubs that frame townhouses and garden-style apartments with a mix of brick and siding exteriors, tricycles are parked neatly next to patio doors, and sidewalks are spotless.

At the development's administrative center, which serves as a focal point for the community, the daycare rooms are filled with light, and their walls are covered with youngsters' colorful drawings. Outside, the pool is ready for swimmers to arrive later in the afternoon. Children are running around the playground, and when they spot Richard Baron, they sprint over for lots of hugs, shouting their greetings and giggling.

To them, he is not a nationally acclaimed developer of affordable housing. He is someone who has given them a fun place to grow up. Baron has also helped give their parents hope, a stake in this community. The committed urban pioneer—who stoops during a conversation to pick up a lone piece of litter from a yard—does not just build low-income rental units. He does not just build profitable mixed-income housing developments. He is determined to build a better way of life in neighborhoods nationwide.

Baron is cofounder, chairman, and chief executive officer of McCormack Baron Salazar (MBS) in St. Louis, a for-profit firm that specializes in the development of economically integrated urban neighborhoods, most of which were formerly disinvested communities. "What has sustained me over the years are the stories of families whose lives have been turned around, the stories of children who are in a better place, whose parents are in job training," Baron says. "The pleasure I get out of this comes from being involved in the turnaround of these communities, of making a difference in people's lives."

The first phase of Murphy Park opened in 1998, the last phase of the 445-unit development opened last year. With a combination of public housing, subsidized units, and market-rate units, monthly rents range from about $150 to $750. It is now a great place to live, report residents, who add that years ago, the neighborhood was hellish. It

"What has sustained me over the years are the stories of families who are in a better place. The pleasure I get out of this comes from being involved in the turnaround of these communities, of making a difference in people's lives."

RICHARD D. BARON • 2004 NICHOLS LAUREATE

was situated across from the city's infamous Pruitt-Igoe public housing project, had high rises that were in deplorable shape, and was named, ironically, for attorney George L. Vaughn, a civil rights activist who fought against the very type of segregated, isolated living conditions that public housing fostered. (In 1948, Vaughn was involved in the U.S. Supreme Court landmark case *Shelly v. Kramer* in which the court struck down restrictive state covenants denying the sale of real estate to African Americans.)

"It was horrible here," affirms Marlene Hodges, a Murphy Park resident and community activist who lived in the Vaughn housing complex. "Parts of it were abandoned, there was a lot of crime, and there were no activities for the youth or families. If not for Richard, there's no telling what would be going on here right now. He came in, and now we're living side by side, instead of stacked on top of each other. The neighbors interact, and people love where they live," she continues.

In many ways, Murphy Park exemplifies the total turnaround that Baron and MBS have been able to achieve in neighborhoods nationwide. Since 1973, MBS has developed more than 11,500 units of affordable and market-rate housing in 100 developments in 25 cities across the United States, including Kansas City; Cleveland; Pittsburgh; Los Angeles; San Francisco; Phoenix; Fort Worth; Atlanta; Richmond, Virginia; Minneapolis; Highland Park, Michigan; New Haven, Connecticut; and New York City. Most of the projects are rentals, although the firm has incorporated some for-sale housing in its developments. All of the rental properties, as well as 5,000 other properties nationwide, are managed by MBS.

Although the residences—which incorporate many green building features—are well designed and well built, the housing itself is only half of the MBS story. The second half has to do with MBS's emphasis on connecting residents with social services they need to succeed in life—such as job training, child care, after-school programs, youth activities, and elder care. It is a holistic approach to community development that stems from the company's mission: "to rebuild neighborhoods in central cities that have deteriorated through decades of neglect and disinvestment."

This longtime dedication to transform blighted areas into thriving living environments has resulted in Baron's selection as the fifth annual laureate of the ULI J.C. Nichols Prize for Visionaries in Urban Development. The $100,000 prize is named for legendary Kansas City, Missouri, developer Jesse Clyde Nichols, a founding member of the Institute.

Peter S. Rummell, chairman and chief executive officer of the St. Joe Company in Jacksonville, Florida, chaired the jury that selected Baron as the Nichols prize recipient. The selection of the 62-year-old urban pioneer highlights a key element of community building—affordable housing—and adds to the variety of design and development aspects celebrated by the prize, Rummell explains. "Richard represents a very important body of work, and he has done it well over a long period of time. He has shown that developing affordable housing can be both the right thing to do and good business."

In addition to Rummell, other jury members were Joseph E. Brown, president and chief executive officer of EDAW Inc., in San Francisco; Ronald Ratner, president of the Forest City Residential Group Inc., in Cleveland; A. Eugene Kohn, chairman of Kohn

Pedersen Fox Associates PC in New York City; and Robert Campbell, architecture critic for the *Boston Globe.*

"Richard Baron's long-term impact is successfully demonstrating the benefits of inclusivity in neighborhoods and showing that diversity makes for a rich environment," notes jury member Ratner. "Housing patterns have long been determined by race and income, but he is a shining example of how that can be changed. Rewarding Richard Baron with the Nichols prize gives a well-rounded picture of what it takes to make great places."

Baron's devotion to building high-quality live/work/play/learn environments stemmed from a stint in 1963 as a school volunteer in Cleveland's Hough neighborhood, an area torn up by poverty and neglect. (Years later, MBS would develop Lexington Village, a thriving community in Hough.) After graduating with a law degree from the University of Michigan, Baron settled in St. Louis, representing public housing tenants for the Legal Aid Society. In the 1970s, he met homebuilder Terry McCormack, and the two teamed up to form McCormack Baron & Associates. "We had $1,000 in the bank, but we were determined," Baron says with a chuckle.

McCormack died suddenly in 1981. Whereas the firm has since expanded from a single building to a multiblock development, it has never strayed from McCormack and Baron's original mission—to regenerate blighted neighborhoods. McCormack's son, Kevin, who joined the firm in 1981, is now the president of MBS in St. Louis, and Tony Salazar, who has been with the firm since 1985, is president of the MBS office in Los Angeles. In 2003, Baron changed the company's name from McCormack Baron & Associates to McCormack Baron Salazar.

"Richard will come to L.A. to look at a possible project and we'll walk around and kick the dirt and look at things. Richard immediately begins to pick out the site's salient features, how the street pattern hooks into surrounding neighborhoods, special buildings that can be saved to establish a special character for a project . . . how future residents can access community activities. He immediately starts to blend all these impressions into a plan," Salazar says.

> *"Richard Baron's long-term impact is successfully demonstrating the benefits of inclusivity in neighborhoods and showing that diversity makes for a rich environment."*
>
> RONALD RATNER • 2004 JURY MEMBER

Another example of MBS's work in St. Louis is Westminster Place, a striking neighborhood with rich architecture, but which for years was cursed with horrendous crime. MBS revived it by developing a retail center, single-family homes, townhouses, and street landscaping. Its success drew other developers, and today, construction is going strong. "We've gone into areas where you would not drive during the day," Baron says. "I see our firm as an agent of change. We set out to change the economics of communities and empower families."

Thomas Reeves, executive director of Downtown Now! in St. Louis, a public/private partnership created to implement the city's downtown redevelopment plan, recalls meeting Baron in the early 1980s, when Baron was developing Quality Hill in Kansas City. At the time, Reeves, a loan officer at Mark Twain Bank (which participated in the project financing), was skeptical but intrigued by what Baron was attempting in an area most people chose to overlook. "He has incredible vision, in that he can walk into a devastated area and see it for what it can be," Reeves says.

Rather than calculating rents based on development costs, Baron "builds the equation backward" by first determining rents. Then, based on development costs, he fills in the funding not covered by equity and traditional financing with funding pieced together from public and philanthropic sources, Reeves explains. "It is an extremely hard approach, but he does it well."

Baron estimates that MBS has raised $65 million in gap financing for its projects, which, to date, total more than $1.4 billion in development costs. "The process of building communities, in many respects, involves a combination of the business and philanthropic community working together," he says. While the firm considers strong public support a necessity in its endeavors, politics is rarely an obstacle, Baron says. "Almost everyone, regardless of their political affiliation, wants their communities to be more livable."

The success of MBS's developments hinges on the success of mixed-income housing—in most of the projects, between 50 and 60 percent of the units are reserved for low- and moderate-income families. But Baron takes great care to ensure that his units appeal to those paying full rents. "We've had to create a way for market-rate families to feel they are benefiting from relocating to one of our developments," he says. Because the communities are all in close-in neighborhoods, they are drawing many professionals who are seeking to reduce their commutes and live closer to downtown amenities.

"The issue of economic integration is an issue that revolves around values, not incomes. When families share a desire for their kids to succeed, economic integration is not a problem," Baron says. "We have individuals earning six figures living next to minimum-wage families, and it works fine."

Baron's firm belief in the positive impact of mixed-income housing led to a fundamental change in the implementation of the federal government's HOPE VI (Housing Opportunities for People Everywhere) housing program. Enacted in 1992, the legislation creating the program authorized grants to be distributed through the U.S. Department of Housing and Urban Development (HUD) to public housing authorities to replace distressed public housing with revitalized projects. However, because the legislation aimed only at project

Opposite:

Top: A fun place to play and learn; the tot lot outside of Murphy Park's daycare center in St. Louis. *(MBS)*

Bottom right: In 1973, Baron *(right)* and McCormack *(center)* talk with a resident of the Pruitt-Igoe public housing project in St. Louis. *(MBS)*

Bottom left: Ready for swimmers: the community pool at Atlanta's Centennial Place. *(MBS)*

replacement, Baron saw that it did not address the issues of project isolation and segregation that often kept public housing tenants in a downward spiral.

In 1993, Baron worked with HUD Secretary Henry Cisneros and his chief of staff, Bruce Katz, to issue HOPE VI regulations permitting mixed-income housing to be part of the public housing redevelopment projects. Baron knew that the ability to include market-rate units would draw other sources of funding, greatly leveraging the HOPE VI grants, and he knew that mixing tenants of various incomes would result in far more stable neighborhoods.

"He came in with twin propositions to make economic integration a program goal and to leverage substantial investment. It is highly unusual for a for-profit developer to have that kind of impact on policy making," says Katz, now a vice president and the founding director of the Metropolitan Policy Program at the Brookings Institution in Washington, D.C. Cisneros, as the former mayor of San Antonio, immediately recognized the potential of Baron's proposals, Katz notes. "Together, they changed the program, and it has made a major difference in some of the toughest communities."

The program changes "introduced a new way for public housing authorities to think about public housing in America," says Cisneros, now chief executive officer of American CityVista in San Antonio. "They started thinking in terms of bonding capacity and using new debt instruments." The private sector involvement in HOPE VI resulting from Baron's concept "has been a hallmark of the program. It's the reason it has been so successful," Cisneros explains.

Since 1992, HUD has awarded more than 440 HOPE VI grants totaling nearly $5.4 billion—and has leveraged billions more—in more than 160 cities. However, the Bush administration has proposed eliminating funding for the program, citing long delays between grant awards and the completion of the revitalization projects at many sites. "In some cases, the funds have not been executed in a timely fashion, and that is a real cause for criticism. But let's not throw the baby out with the bathwater. If the program needs to be recalibrated, let's do it," Baron says.

The HOPE VI change Baron sought was rooted in his experience with mixed-income housing at Murphy Park in St. Louis, which became the prototype for the federal program. Jefferson Elementary School in Murphy Park also became the model for another key focus of Baron's developments—which is to use schools as a focal point for the surrounding community. A few years ago, Jefferson's library was locked, its gym equipment was broken or missing, and the school had no computers. With no air conditioning, the students sweltered. Moreover, although the school was within easy walking distance to Murphy Park and an adjacent neighborhood, most of its students were bused in from other parts of St. Louis.

Baron convinced the city school board to let him undertake an overhaul, provided that Jefferson would be a neighborhood school. He raised $3.5 million from 20 corporations, which was used to install a central air conditioning system, purchase computers for administrative and student use, purchase new gym equipment, refurbish the library, and improve the building's interior and exterior. Today, the neighborhood children walk to school, and their learning levels have improved dramatically. Baron's success with Jefferson led

A streetscape at Crawford Square in Pittsburgh's revived Hill District. *(MBS)*

Educating for Change

One of Richard Baron's favorite quotes is from baseball pitching star Satchel Paige: "Never look back because someone may be gaining on you." However—largely to Baron's dismay—he realizes he still has few competitors in the business of large-scale affordable housing development. In frustration, he sometimes tells his staff, "We've been looking back for 30 years and there's nobody there."

As a result, Baron is working to cultivate a new generation of land use practitioners who are willing to apply a holistic approach to neighborhood development and who see the long-term value of providing both affordable housing and social infrastructure to give new life to withering communities. He turned a concept he first raised in a speech a few years ago into the Center for Urban Redevelopment Excellence (CURExPenn), now in its second year at the University of Pennsylvania. Funded with a $2.4 million grant from the John S. and James L. Knight Foundation, the program aims to train more than 400 urban development professionals in the skills necessary to develop thriving urban neighborhoods.

Those selected to participate as program fellows start with six weeks of intensive training at the University of Pennsylvania, which includes topics such as large-scale real estate development and financing; high-quality urban design and planning based on strong market assessment; roles of different redevelopment partners; race, gender, and class issues; and leadership. After that, the fellows are placed for two years with sponsor organizations that generally specialize in large-scale real estate development in distressed areas. Fellows work as project managers at the host companies, and they are mentored by the senior staff.

Eleven people were selected for the first group of CURExPenn fellows. They are between the ages of 26 and 47, and their career backgrounds range from social service work to law. The program generally attracts people "early in their careers who are looking to make a change," says executive director Valerie Piper. "It's not an age thing, it's a stage thing. They are at a point in their lives where they want to make a change and have not yet found a way to make a serious transition," she says. "They are doers. They are not afraid of risk. They come from all different backgrounds, and they are willing to move, learn, and in some cases, take a substantial pay cut. But they all share an incredible commitment to social change. We hope that a few more Richard Barons will graduate from this program."

Urban planner Julie DeGraaf is a CURExPenn fellow placed at McCormack Baron Salazar. Formerly working for a community development corporation in Chicago, she wanted to learn more about housing and community development on a larger scale, and the program at Penn seemed like the perfect fit. "It has given me an opportunity to dig deeper into what I am interested in," says DeGraaf. "I like being part of something that sets the standards for the way I think neighborhoods should be built."

For Baron, CURExPenn represents a way to attract to the community development industry the best and the brightest young professionals—those with a social conscience and an entrepreneurial streak. "My hope is that the program will develop a new class of entrepreneurs who are committed to seeing these projects through, to making these communities happen," he says. "The real challenge is how to take those interested in entrepreneurship and get them involved in doing this type of work. The more we get information out—through an education and mentoring process—the faster we can change communities across the United States and the world. We want to educate those who have a fire in their bellies, who don't want to go into social or educational work, but into community development. The whole idea is to do good and do well." ∎

to his spearheading the revitalization of the city's Adams Elementary School and, ultimately, to the creation of the Vashon Education Compact, a partnership between the St. Louis public schools in the city's inner neighborhoods and the corporate, civic, and philanthropic community. Also, he is working with school boards in other communities in which MBS is developing projects.

"The relationship between schools and neighborhoods is understood well in suburban communities, but not in urban areas. That needs to change," Baron says. "The focus we (MBS) have on upgrading schools is designed to help children coming out of lower-income families to succeed, while at the same time, it creates new resources to attract new buyers who will invest in these communities."

In St. Louis, Baron's knack for visioning also is apparent outside of his housing developments. MBS developed a Westin Hotel at Cupples Station, a series of historic brick warehouses once used to store goods and serve the railroad running through the city. The firm also transformed a former synagogue in a building designed by Eric Mendelsohn into the Center of Creative Arts (COCA), the city's largest multidisciplinary arts institution. COCA's programs include performances in its 400-seat theater; educational classes, camps, and workshops serving children and adults; artists' residences; exhibits of contemporary art in the Anheuser-Busch Gallery; and an extensive outreach program offered to low-income youth through its nationally recognized urban arts program. Of all MBS's endeavors, COCA "has stolen my heart," Baron admits.

"His support for the city goes way beyond development projects," says Richard Fleming, president and chief executive officer of the St. Louis Regional Chamber and Growth Association. Fleming points to MBS's initiative in the Choteau Lake and Greenway

SINCE RECEIVING THE NICHOLS PRIZE IN 2004

Richard Baron has guided McCormack Baron Salazar (MBS) to develop an additional 5,694 units of housing and 351,742 square feet of commercial space, totaling $1.4 billion in development investment ($2.9 billion since 1973). When Baron was selected the Nichols Prize winner, the recognition was largely due to MBS's development philosophy of rebuilding neighborhoods through high-quality, economically integrated housing and of improving the performance of neighborhood schools. In the ten intervening years, MBS has expanded its focus to an even more holistic approach that includes development of human capital; environmentally sustainable buildings and communities; improved access to transit; and commercial, retail, and service development.

Just as Baron was instrumental in implementing the federal government's HOPE VI program, enacted in 1992, he was equally instrumental in the creation of the Choice Neighborhood program, introduced in 2010 by the U.S. Department of Housing and Urban Development (HUD) to facilitate a comprehensive approach to neighborhood transformation. The Choice program builds off the lessons of public housing transformation learned from HOPE VI and expands the focus from addressing just distressed public housing sites. The program seeks to transform high poverty, distressed neighborhoods into neighborhoods with healthy, affordable housing; well-functioning services; high-quality public education programs and services; public assets; public transportation; and improved access to jobs. To date, MBS has been a member of teams

The Quality Hill neighborhood in Kansas City. In 1985, MBS began a rehabilitation and new construction development creating more than 300 apartments and condominiums and thousands of square feet of commercial space. "I see our firm as an agent of change. We set out to change the economics of communities and empower families," Baron says. (MBS)

Project, which aims to restore a part of the historic Choteau Lake bed as a water feature. The greenway component will redevelop abandoned railways as an urban park trail system that will extend outward from the Gateway Arch to the city's Forest Park. "It will be a wonderful city amenity, and it was Richard who first brought it to our attention. His vision is contagious," Fleming says. Baron, he notes, is a "rare individual" whose combination of "vision, entrepreneurialism, and social justice is built into everything he does."

Says St. Louis Mayor Francis G. Slay: "What he does is not for show. He is not in the business just to make money. He really cares about people. There are a lot of good developers here, but I would not put anyone next to him."

that have been awarded five $30 million Choice Neighborhood Implementation Grants and two Choice Neighborhoods Planning Grants in cities across the United States.

On the energy and sustainability side, MBS, under the direction of Baron, has installed more than 2.6 megawatts of solar power generation at 28 sites. Four MBS communities—two under construction and two completed—have been certified under the Leadership in Energy and Environmental Design (LEED) for Neighborhood Development program. In addition, MBS has developed 30 green developments, with certifications from the U.S. Green Building Council, Enterprise Green Communities, and HUD Green Communities.

MBS has also worked to use the New Markets Tax Credit (NMTC) Program to invest in developments that complement housing with needed commercial investments. In total, MBS has received NMTC allocations of $220 million since 2006. With investments in 27 projects, more than $659 million has been leveraged in these deals.

Baron continues to serve on the executive committee of the St. Louis, Missouri, Regional Chamber and Growth Association and on the boards of the Partnership for Downtown St. Louis, Downtown Now!, and COCA, the Center of Creative Arts. ∎

ALBERT B. RATNER AND FOREST CITY ENTERPRISES INC.

When "Good" Is Not Enough

Originally published in October 2005

Opposite: Central Station in Chicago, a mixed-use development of offices, for-sale condominiums, and rental apartments spanning 80 acres, is just minutes from the heart of Chicago's Loop.

To describe Cleveland-based Forest City Enterprises Inc. as a good company is accurate, but it seems hardly adequate. Since 1921, when the firm got its start building and selling two-car garages—guaranteed not to leak—for $179.50, it has grown exponentially into a highly respected $7.4 billion real estate development organization with close to 300 projects in nearly 150 communities in 20 states.

Yet, despite Forest City's extraordinary streak of success in community building, "good" is precisely the description that cochairman Albert B. Ratner uses to sum up the company's work. "We don't have a great company, we have a good company, and we are trying to be better. Once you are a great company, what else is there to do? There are a lot of things we have to do that we don't even know about."

This modesty is typical of Ratner, who clearly has played a leading role in Forest City's myriad contributions to America's urban areas. His lifelong dedication to creating positive change in communities through Forest City's developments has earned both Ratner and Forest City the 2005 ULI J.C. Nichols Prize for Visionaries in Urban Development. The prize honors the legacy of ULI founder and legendary Kansas City, Missouri, developer Jesse Clyde Nichols, who built the still-thriving Country Club Plaza and surrounding residential neighborhoods during the first half of the past century.

At 78, Ratner understands the difficulty Nichols and his contemporaries faced in maintaining their real estate businesses during the Great Depression. "What few people understand is that between 1929 and 1950, [the business of] real estate was practically nonexistent. There were people—giants like Nichols—who were there before World War II, who were tremendous builders, and we [current land use professionals] don't really appreciate them. But they made it possible for us to do what we are doing."

He recalls Forest City's own struggle to sell timber during that time—"Maybe we would get pickles for some two-by-fours"—and it instilled in him a sense of humility that remains an important part of the company's makeup.

To shape Forest City's culture of teamwork and collaboration, Ratner has drawn heavily on lessons learned from his parents. "My mother said, 'There is no limit to what

"We have a good company, and we are trying to be better. Once you are a great company, what else is there to do? There are a lot of things we have to do that we don't even know about. . . . Building a great company is a wonderful thing only if other things go with it—a great family and a great community."

ALBERT B. RATNER · 2005 NICHOLS LAUREATE

Left: Sterling Glen of Bay Shore in Bay Shore, New York, a restored Victorian mansion, is one of many distinctive assisted living facilities developed by Forest City Enterprises.

Right: The Promenade in Temecula, a retail development on 75 acres in California's Temecula Valley, located between San Diego and Los Angeles.

you can do if you don't care who gets the credit.' My father said, 'If you remember where you came from, you will always know where you are going,'" he says. "If you combine those two principles, you have not only a good business, but a good life, because you know what's important."

Ratner's brother-in-law, Samuel H. Miller, 84, cochairs Forest City; he has worked with Ratner at the company for nearly 60 years. Both attribute its success to the collective contributions of its employees and outside partnerships. "This company was built by thousands of employees," says Miller, who is also the company's treasurer. "There is no way Al and I could have done this by ourselves. Here, the 'me, me' is out entirely."

Over the years, the company, founded by Albert Ratner's father, two uncles, and an aunt, sold its lumber business and branched into land acquisition and development; retail, office, and residential development; and, ultimately, master-planned development of mixed-use projects. Forest City's developments are in both downtown cores as well as suburban greenfields. Yet, despite the company's extraordinary growth, which was spurred by going public in 1960, Forest City has remained a tightly knit family operation; its website even contains a "family tree" to help sort out the lineup. Among the Ratners: Charles, Albert's cousin, is president and chief executive officer of the company. Cousin Ronald is president and chief executive officer of Forest City Residential Group, Inc.; Ronald's brother and Albert's cousin James is president and chief executive officer of Forest City Commercial Group Inc.; and cousin Bruce is president and chief executive officer, Forest City Ratner Companies. Albert's son Brian is president of East Coast Development for Forest City Enterprises Inc.; and Albert's daughter Debra Ratner Salzberg is president of Forest City Washington, Inc.

However, Albert Ratner is quick to point out that he and his relatives view the term "family" in the broadest sense: when he and Miller decided that Forest City could best gain financial clout by offering company shares to the public, they viewed it as a choice to become a larger company involving a larger number of families. "We always felt this business was big enough, not only for our family members, but for all kinds of family members—fathers, brothers, sisters, daughters. The broader concept of family is very important to us," he says.

"The family is much larger than the bloodline—it really is a family of people working together, and that is not just rhetoric," says James Ratner. "It is an atmosphere in which people can say what they want and talk things out honestly. The inspiration for this comes from Albert. He is very direct and unambiguous."

Backing up employees when they err is as critical to Albert Ratner as giving them credit when they succeed. "When things are going good, I don't hear from Al too much, but when things go bad, I know he will be there," says Ronald Ratner. "That is when he is at his most supportive best."

Explains Albert: "We really are not second-guessers. We expect mistakes to be made. We give people a lot of responsibility and authority, because we believe creativity can only flourish in that kind of environment. And we need a much larger group of creative people than most companies might need, because we do so many things in so many places."

Forest City's flexibility is illustrated by its wide variety of developments, ranging from Metrotech Center in Brooklyn, a 16-acre office campus that is one of the largest

> "They [Albert Ratner and Forest City Enterprises] look at the tough places, where there is no market. They have shown that they can be ahead of trends and can reshape the market in not just one location, but in different locations."
>
> JOSEPH E. BROWN • 2005 JURY CHAIR

developments in New York City; to University Park, a mixed-use complex at the Massachusetts Institute of Technology in Cambridge (the project was a 2004 ULI Awards for Excellence winner); to Ohana Military Communities near Honolulu, a modernization of military family housing in Hawaii. Certainly, Stapleton in Denver, the transformation of the city's former airport into a 4,700-acre multipurpose community, and Terminal Tower, the renovation of Cleveland's most famous building, rank among Forest City's best-known endeavors. In a brilliant example of "out-of-the-box" thinking, the company hired celebrity photographer Annie Leibovitz to document its construction of the 52-story New York Times building in New York City. Forest City will display the photos—a series of both close-ups and panoramic shots—in a public gallery outside the site.

However, Forest City's roster of work contains smaller projects in addition to the larger ones, many of which are in edgy inner-city neighborhoods of both strong and weaker cities. "They look at the tough places, where there is no market," says 2005 Nichols Prize jury chair Joseph E. Brown, president and chief executive officer of EDAW Inc. in San Francisco. "They go in and create markets for housing, office, and retail, and they believe in what they can do. Considering all the components needed to make it work … it is not easy. But they have shown that they can be ahead of trends and can reshape the market in not just one location, but in different locations."

STAPLETON, COLORADO

"We've Learned a Lot"

When completed, Stapleton is projected to include 8,000 houses, 4,000 apartments, four schools, and 2 million square feet of retail space. *(Trepal Photography Inc.)*

Forest City Enterprises' $4 billion redevelopment of Denver's Stapleton International Airport—currently the largest infill development in the United States—is a study in building partnerships and overcoming challenges. When the company was selected in 1998 to be the master developer, it was chosen to turn seven square miles of concrete into an environmentally conscious, pedestrian-friendly, new urbanist community with ample green space. To do this, Forest City is coordinating the work of more than a dozen homebuilders, scores of architects and engineers, and hundreds of contractors. It also has created public/private partnerships to secure financing for $600 million in infrastructure. When the massive makeover is completed, it will include 8,000 homes and 4,000 apartments, 13 million square feet of office and retail space, two elementary schools, four middle schools, two high schools, and several preschool learning facilities.

The community emphasizes sustainable building, which is in keeping with the Stapleton Development Plan, known as the "Green Book," created in 1995 by the Stapleton Redevelopment Foundation to address the physical design and economic, environmental, and social objectives of the community. All of Stapleton's homes are required to meet sustainability standards set by Built Green Colorado, an organization that encourages energy conservation and natural resource preservation in development. The development has won several awards for sustainability, including the 2004 Best in American Living Award for Smart Growth from the National Association of Home Builders. It also won the Stockholm Partnerships for Sustainable Cities Award in 2002 and an Environmental Achievement Award in 2004 from the Colorado Department of Public Health and Environment. In 2001, Stapleton was recognized as a model community by the United Nations Council on Sustainable Development.

"It is highly unusual for a development company to embrace sustainability in such a comprehensive way," says Terrell J. Minger, president and chief executive officer of the Center for Resource Management, with offices in Denver and Salt Lake City. The center, dedicated to environmental problem solving, crafted the Green Book's section on sustainable design and green building criteria for Stapleton. Whereas the Green Book provided a guide, Forest City—which had little experience with sustainable building before Stapleton—"really pushed it [sustainable building] forward" and offered new ideas to maximize green building practices, Minger says. "I don't know of another major developer that applies this level of sensitivity at this scale." He points out that Forest City has managed to take all the elements of the Green Book and "weave them together intelligently. . . . Every year, Stapleton gets better."

Today, with more than 2,000 homes completed, nearly 5,000 people are living in Stapleton. According to Tom Gleason, vice president of public relations for Forest City Stapleton Inc., the community's emphasis on sustainability and recreation appeals to Denver's health-conscious residents. One of the old airport hangars has already been converted into a health club and recreational facility. Nearly 30 percent of Stapleton's acreage is reserved for parks and open space, including the 80-acre Central Park, which will feature skateboard parks and sledding hills. A bike and trail system meanders through the community and links to the Rocky Mountain Arsenal National Wildlife Refuge. The homes, shops, and offices at Stapleton are all connected by narrow streets, designed to encourage walking and minimize car use: even its big-box retail stores are designed to be accessible on foot. "People in Denver like the outdoors, and they respect open space," Gleason says, recounting how needless it was to reserve parking for attendees at Stapleton's first Founder's Day celebration. "We had a crowd, but nobody drove. We had a stroller jam."

Gleason says the community's diversity, in terms of demographics, architecture, lifestyle, and income, is another draw: the housing is mixed, with homes priced in the $100,000s positioned across the street from those selling for $1 million. Currently, most of the people buying in Stapleton are from established in-town neighborhoods, he says. Perhaps the most telling testament to Stapleton's impact is the fact that one of its first residents moved from a neighborhood directly across the street from the development. "He had grown up with the noise of jets taking off right over his roof, and he wanted to be in on the good things going on here now," Gleason says.

The transformation of Stapleton has spanned terms of three mayors: Federico Peña, who was mayor when the airport closing was announced in 1989; Wellington Webb, who oversaw the crafting of the redevelopment plan in 1995 and the initial construction work in 2001; and John W. Hickenlooper, the current mayor, whose administration is working with Forest City to keep the project moving toward completion, set for 2020. Says Hickenlooper, "Forest City is so far ahead of its time. . . . It has been a perfect partner for the city and it delivers on its promises. Cities need companies like Forest City."

"We look at partnerships more as a way to broaden opportunities than to lessen economic risk. The best results happen by collaborating and working with people—it's all about partnerships," says Albert Ratner. "I look back at the old things we did, and people ask, 'Why did you develop that in that way?' Well, that was the knowledge we had at the time. Then I look at Stapleton and say to myself, 'We've learned a lot.'" ∎

100 Landsdowne Street: The Residences at University Park is part of University Park at the Massachusetts Institute of Technology. The entire mixed-use development was chosen as a 2004 ULI Awards for Excellence winner.

In addition to Brown, other Nichols Prize jury members are Robert Campbell, architecture critic for the *Boston Globe*; Bonnie Fisher, principal and director of landscape design at ROMA Design Group in San Francisco; A. Eugene Kohn, president of Kohn Pedersen Fox Associates PC in New York City; and Christopher B. Leinberger, partner at the Arcadia Land Company in Albuquerque and director of a new graduate real estate development program at the University of Michigan. "Cities consider themselves blessed if Forest City comes to town," says Leinberger. "They know how to create a tremendous value through place and how to build a sense of community. They get it. What they do gives us [the development community] legitimacy to try new things."

Andrew Altman, chief executive officer of the city's Anacostia Waterfront Corporation in Washington, D.C., and the city's former planning director, remembers walking around a barren site in Washington's Southeast quadrant four years ago with Albert Ratner and Deborah Ratner Salzberg. They were discussing redevelopment possibilities for the site in conjunction with the city's plans for overall revitalization along Washington's Anacostia River. "There was nothing there, and people were skeptical that anything could happen on it. But Albert saw the potential. He said, 'This is what we love to do,'" Altman recalls. "He understands complex urban redevelopment, and he knows what makes cities exciting." Today, that area in Southeast is undergoing massive rejuvenation, much of which has been triggered by plans to construct a stadium for the Washington Nationals, the city's new major league baseball team.

Forest City's investment in Washington's waterfront spans a vast section near the convergence of the Anacostia and Potomac rivers, and its projects in that area include a mall renovation, affordable housing constructed through the federal HOPE VI program, and new retail and office space. "What distinguishes Forest City is that it doesn't do things piecemeal; it goes in with a commitment to bring back entire neighborhoods," Altman says. "It really embeds itself in the community and has staying power. No challenge is too daunting."

According to James Ratner, Forest City's penchant for iffy locations stretches back three decades and is attributable to Albert Ratner's contrarian nature. "When everyone else said the urban markets of America were places you didn't want to be and that the only place to be was in the suburbs, Albert took exactly the opposite tack," he says. "The trick is not to go where everyone else is going; the trick is to have the foresight to understand where people will go if you can create the place."

Forest City's rejuvenation of Terminal Tower took nearly ten years to complete. Built in 1928 with marble, granite, and cherrywood framing its majestic public space, it had fallen into disrepair over the years, reflecting the disinvestment that had occurred throughout America's downtowns following World War II. When Forest City acquired the building in 1983 and began the slow, meticulous restoration process, most of Cleveland's inner core was "decaying" and "there was disbelief, because it had been so long since any investment had occurred," says Joseph D. Roman, president and chief executive officer of the Greater Cleveland Partnership (GCP), which promotes economic development in that city. He met Albert Ratner about 20 years ago, when both were charter members of

Cleveland Tomorrow, the forerunner of GCP. At the time, creating a physically appealing downtown was not a priority for many of the business executives in the group, Roman remembers. "Albert fixed that by making sure the organization understood that the way the city looked and felt was just as central to what we were trying to do with job creation as anything else on our agenda. . . . He is one of those people who just doesn't give up. He believes the city is capable of anything. Today, people realize that growth in the central city is not only possible, it's happening," Roman says.

The $600 million redevelopment of the Terminal Tower and the former Union Terminal into Tower City Center, along with the addition of new office buildings, a first-class hotel, and retail stores, has made the 6.5 million-square-foot project a thriving section of Cleveland. The project, which includes a regional shopping mall, the M-K Ferguson Plaza building, the Skylight office tower, the Ritz-Carlton hotel and office tower, and a new rapid transit station, opened in 1990.

"Forest City's investment in Tower City made all the other investments—the Rock and Roll Hall of Fame, the Gateway District (a historic neighborhood of restaurants, clubs, and sports arenas)—happen," says Steve Strnisha, formerly with GCP and now president of Strnisha Development Advisors in Cleveland. "Now, all Clevelanders know the center of the city. Forest City is significant because it is big and because it cares. It has not forgotten its hometown."

The company's decision to move ahead with the tower refurbishment was based on its philosophy that "change takes time," Albert Ratner explains. "We believed this project could make money for the company, and that it could change Cleveland, which would be good for the company." He notes two key offshoots of the project—greater credibility with other communities regarding the company's commitment to tackle tough deals and a greater understanding of public/private partnerships.

Creating long-lasting, mutually beneficial partnerships with the public sector and other private companies is a longstanding tradition at Forest City, says Charles Ratner. "We are not really a real estate development company, we are a community development company. We believe strongly in relationships with both the private and public sectors in every community we work in," he says, pointing to the company's success in Brooklyn with Metrotech. "We don't just do a project in New York City. We do community development in New York City with New York City as our partner. To stay in the business, your projects have to work financially and work for the community as well. We created a way to save jobs for Brooklyn. But if we could not have made a competitive return, we could not have built an environment to create new jobs and attract new capital and investment into the community."

Adds Ronald Ratner: "The business of making money is not at odds with community interests. You can't be part of a community if you are only looking at quarterly reports," he says. "Albert's legacy is that you can bring integrity into real estate. He has shown that development can be a profession that can have a positive impact and that there does not have to be an adversarial relationship with the community."

Albert Ratner's son, Brian Ratner, says his father has instilled in him, and all the company's employees, the importance of respecting relationships. "Some of them [the

Forest City's $600 million redevelopment of the Terminal Tower and the former Union Terminal into Tower City Center, along with the addition of new office buildings, a first-class hotel, and retail stores, has made the 6.5 million-square-foot project the centerpiece of a thriving section of downtown Cleveland.

Members of the Ratner family accept the National
Building Museum's Honor Award for 2005.

business relationships] are older than I am," says the 48-year-old. "I believe our company
stands out in that regard. People know our word is gold. We don't overcommit. We say
what we are going to do and we do it."

"When I started in the business and was out making a deal, I would come back to
the office and the first question my father and uncle would ask me was not 'Did you make
the deal?' It was, 'How is our reputation?'" recalls Albert Ratner. "They believed that if we
had our reputation, it could only help us make another deal. . . . Being the boss means
you take responsibility to see that the company is making money, but that it is making
money with people, not off people.

"I don't like to compare what we have done with other companies. What we've done
works for us," Ratner says. "If people say to me, 'You've built this great business,' to me,
that is no big deal. It is a wonderful thing [only] if other things go with it—a great family
and a great community."

According to Hilel Lewis, director and founder of the Cole Eye Institute in Cleveland,
an outstanding example of Albert Ratner's commitment to the community is his strong
support of Vision First, which provides free sight screenings to Cleveland public school
district students in prekindergarten, kindergarten, and first grade. "He saw this program
as a way to combine his commitment to high-quality education with his commitment to
high-quality health care," Lewis says.

Lewis, who has known Ratner for about ten years, has worked closely with him on
several community-oriented projects, and considers him one of his closest friends. "He is
the most respected civic leader in the city. . . . He is unselfish, wise, and humble. When I
need good advice, I call Albert. He listens, he thinks creatively, and he reasons logically."

"I don't want to be remembered for building a business," says Ratner. "I just want
those people whose lives I have affected to remember me, because I am made up of the
memories of all those people who helped me."

SINCE RECEIVING THE NICHOLS PRIZE IN 2005

Albert B. Ratner and Forest City Enterprises Inc. have continued to develop innovative projects throughout the United States; the company's assets currently total about $9 billion.

Over the past decade, Forest City has executed dozens of projects—some notable projects include the New York Times Building in New York City, which provides premium office space for the storied newspaper; 8 Spruce Street in New York City (also known as New York by Gehry), a residential building designed by celebrated architect Frank Gehry that has a public school and an ambulatory care center in the lower levels; and the Yards, a mixed-use development along the Anacostia River in the Capitol Riverfront Business Improvement District in Washington, D.C., that features retail, residential, recreational, and office space.

In a 2012 interview for *Urban Land* magazine, Ratner said of the Yards, "That development will change everything around it, including an important part of Washington's inner city and the Anacostia neighborhoods across the river. That's the kind of development that restores cities; it's much more important than spoiling the countryside with outdated sprawl." The Yards' open space feature—Yards Park—won ULI's Urban Open Space Award in 2013.

Another notable Forest City project is Pacific Park Brooklyn (formerly Atlantic Yards), a 22-acre mixed-use development in downtown Brooklyn, New York. The project includes residential and commercial space, as well as the Barclays Center arena. The arena opened in 2012, and the next phase of the project is set to open in late 2015. Most recently, Forest City and Shanghai-based Greenland Group formed a joint venture to accelerate development of this project. Also since 2005, Forest City has dramatically expanded its military housing program, signing 50-year partnerships with the U.S. Navy and Air Force.

The year 2011 brought a unique change to the company's management structure when David LaRue—a 25-year veteran of Forest City—became the first chief executive officer without familial ties to the founding Ratner family. Al Ratner, 86, continues to serve as cochairman emeritus of Forest City alongside Samuel H. Miller and maintains an office in Forest City's Cleveland headquarters.

After receiving the Nichols Prize, Al Ratner and his family requested that ULI apply the $100,000 prize honorarium, along with a personal match of $100,000, to help fund the Institute's efforts to assist Gulf Coast communities in the aftermath of Hurricane Katrina. In the months following the storm, ULI Advisory Services panels visited New Orleans and several communities in Mississippi and Alabama, offering recommendations on rebuilding in a way that would help promote economic prosperity and environmental stability. *(Daniel Lobo)*

Ratner remains committed to the Greater Cleveland community, serving on the advisory board for a local nonprofit, Shoes and Clothes for Kids, and on the advisory committee of the Rock and Roll Hall of Fame Foundation. Since 2012, Ratner has served on Ohio's Executive Workforce Board. He also serves as a governor for the Henry M. Jackson Foundation, is an honorary trustee of Enterprise Foundation, and has long served on the board of trustees for United Jewish Communities.

U.S. Rep. Marcy Kaptur of Ohio honored Ratner on his 85th birthday in a speech on the floor of the U.S. House of Representatives: "He [Al Ratner] epitomizes 'a life well lived.' He is a corporate and community leader with boundless energy who has made an indelible contribution to the Greater Cleveland community," she said. "Not known to mince words, his insights, advice, and counsel are sought broadly. He is always willing to assist, to lead, and to care."

Forest City Enterprises Inc. is just six years shy of celebrating its centennial—a tremendous accomplishment for this real estate stronghold, showcasing its permanence in the industry. ■

2006

PETER CALTHORPE

New Urbanist Pioneer

Originally published in October 2006

Opposite: Homes in Stapleton border a pocket park. "For each project," says Calthorpe, "I ask myself, 'Is it diverse? Is it walkable? Does it restore and protect critical qualities? How does it interconnect and add to the region as a whole?'" *(Forest City Stapleton)*

On what should have been a clear California day in the mid-1960s, 16-year-old Peter Calthorpe was sitting on a hilltop near his home in Palo Alto. His view of the neighborhoods below was completely blocked by smog from automobile emissions. It was a seminal moment. That is when it hit him that something needed to change about the way his hometown—and a lot of other towns—were growing.

"Those were the days when subdivisions wiped out all the orchards where I grew up, and I realized that what was replacing them was not healthy," recalls Calthorpe, now 57. "I didn't know what to do, but I knew I wanted to do something." What began as a teenager's passion to "save the environment" evolved into a 30-year career in urban planning and design, devoted to the creation of communities that are as easily negotiated on foot as by car and that significantly improve the balance between land development and land preservation. Today, Calthorpe, principal of Calthorpe Associates, an architecture, urban design, and urban planning firm in Berkeley, California, is widely regarded as one of the nation's most influential urban designers, improving the growth patterns of communities from coast to coast and overseas. And with John Fregonese, his partner in Fregonese, Calthorpe Associates in Portland, Oregon, he has pioneered the emerging field of regional design.

Since Calthorpe formed Calthorpe Associates in 1983, its work has expanded incrementally to include more than 30 new community designs, among them Stapleton in Denver, Issaquah Highlands in the state of Washington, and Daybreak in Salt Lake City; countless urban revitalization plans, ranging from HOPE VI public housing projects in Chicago to a transit village in Richmond, California; 11 long-term regional plans such as Envision Utah, the COMPAS plan for southern California, and Metro Vision 2040 in Portland, Oregon; and an increasing number of international plans, ranging from the Tunis waterfront to the rural lands of Rotterdam in the Netherlands.

In Calthorpe's view, the business of urban design is the business of creating positive change. "My goal has been to work on projects that, in some serious way, lead to redirecting and repairing the missteps that we in design and development have made since World War II," he says.

"*People are desperate for a sense of community and place. When generic places are created, people are left with unconscious needs and wants—needs that can only be satisfied with more coherent communities. I think constantly about how to bring that about.*"

PETER CALTHORPE · 2006 NICHOLS LAUREATE

Calthorpe believes that urban revitalization and infill development are necessary in both suburban and city locations. An example of suburban infill is the Bay Meadows *(left)* redevelopment in San Mateo, California, which combines the 1 million-square-foot headquarters for Franklin Fund with housing, retail uses, parks, and offices. Oakland, California's urban center needed more diverse housing, which the Uptown project in Oakland *(right)* will provide with about 1,000 units. *(Calthorpe Associates, left and right)*

Although Calthorpe's designs vary broadly according to a project's size and type, all of them are rooted in four principles: providing for diversity, building to human scale, focusing on restoring and preserving buildings, and taking a regional perspective. He constantly weighs his idealistic desire to stay true to those principles against the extent to which they can be fulfilled with each project. But as the development community has increased its overall acceptance of concentrated, mixed-use, mixed-income, pedestrian-oriented design, it has become less challenging for Calthorpe to apply his principles. "We can go a lot further [promoting them] today than we could 15 years ago," he explains. "Developers are finding that design matters and that these principles work. A lot of them now understand how to create value out of building great human places." Calthorpe explains the four principles:

- **On diversity:** "The more diverse, the more complex, the more layered a place is, the better it is. The more segregated, the more isolated, the more segmented a place becomes, the less viable it is."

- **On human scale:** "It's a matter of walkability—of understanding how far a five-minute walk is, at what distance you can recognize someone on the street, how to create environments for people who are moving at five miles per hour rather than 60."

- **On restoration and preservation:** "There is no blank slate. Everywhere you go, there is history—human and natural. Repairing damaged environments and restoring historic human environments have to be part [of design.] Rather than throw away culture, you have to preserve and enhance what is best in a place."

- **On regionalism:** "It's one region against another around the globe. The region is the center stage where people act out their lives—economically, socially, and environmentally—yet, we lack a clear vision for our regions. We tend to let them grow by default or by the sum total of piecemeal actions."

These principles, says Calthorpe, provide direction and guidance. "For each project, I ask myself, 'Is it diverse? Is it walkable? Does it restore and protect critical qualities? How does it interconnect and add to the region as a whole?' Typically, I can find ways to answer each of these questions," he comments.

This lifetime dedication to excellence in urban design has earned Calthorpe the 2006 ULI J.C. Nichols Prize for Visionaries in Urban Development. The $100,000 annual prize, which honors ULI founder and legendary Kansas City developer J.C. Nichols, recognizes an individual whose career demonstrates a commitment to the highest standards of responsible development. Calthorpe, the seventh recipient, is the first architect and first urban designer chosen as a prize laureate. The selection of Calthorpe as this year's laureate honors the work "not only of those who do the developing, but of those who do the planning and who influence planning and development through their ideas and vision," says 2006 Prize jury chair A. Eugene Kohn, chairman of Kohn Pedersen Fox Architects in New York City. "His legacy is one that shows the value of planning cities in an intelligent way." Along with Kohn, other jury members were: Robert Campbell, architectural critic for the *Boston Globe;* Bonnie Fisher, principal, ROMA Design Group, San Francisco; Christopher B. Leinberger, founding partner of the Arcadia Land Company in Albuquerque, New Mexico, and director of a graduate real estate development program at the University of Michigan; and Jeremy Newsum, group chief executive of Grosvenor Estate in London.

As the prize winner, Calthorpe "represents an angle on urban development that often is overlooked," adds jury member Newsum. "Those who plan the way cities should develop are often unsung, but vital to the process. He is at the forefront in a significant movement in redefining how urban areas should work."

Says Calthorpe: "I started from a radical position and I've been lucky enough to take those ideas and make them concrete, make them implementable."

His radical position—favoring compact, walkable, mixed-use, mixed-income, transit-accessible development—stemmed from a stint in the 1970s designing energy-efficient state government buildings in the administration of California Governor Jerry Brown. It was a departure from what Calthorpe had been learning at Yale University, where he cut short his architecture studies. Outside of professors like Vincent Scully (2003 ULI J.C. Nichols Prize laureate), David Sellers, and Charles Moore, who advocated a humanistic approach to architecture, others at the architecture school "were not teaching what I was interested in," Calthorpe says.

"Much of it was focused on the building as an isolated object, and I still see this as a problem in the architectural world. The hyper-modernists see the building as a piece of sculpture that sits in the landscape and not as part of the connective tissue that makes healthy cities and robust urban environments. There is a profound amount of modesty needed to design a building that is just part of the background, part of an urban space, and not an object of its own concern. . . . In my mind, much good architecture is craft, not art, and craft builds on tradition and is unique to each place."

Upon leaving Yale, Calthorpe moved back to the West Coast after being recruited by architect Sim Van der Ryn to work as design director at the Farrollones Institute in the field of climate responsive design. When Van der Ryn took the post as California state architect under Governor Brown, Calthorpe followed, applying his practice to the planning and construction of public buildings. "Features such as natural lighting, passive solar energy, and natural ventilation made for environmentally sound buildings, but how people got the office became a bigger issue, one that opened the field of urban design for me," Calthorpe says.

To encourage access by transit, rather than cars, he and his colleagues opted to omit parking lots from public building design, forcing people to use or at least consider using other ways to get to work besides driving. (Today, the building in Berkeley in which Calthorpe's office is located offers no on-site parking, but it provides lots of bike racks.) This "no parking" approach in Sacramento eventually led to the idea of transit-oriented development. "It became an interlocking set of issues, all with one fundamental premise, which is that people enjoy urban places and being connected to their history and their environment," Calthorpe notes.

Not surprisingly, Calthorpe's urban design concepts were viewed initially with much skepticism: he had the audacity to advocate breaking from the post–World War II pattern of sprawling development planned around suburban highway interchanges and to pursue instead a pattern that more closely resembled pre-World War II layouts using public transit to link home, office, and recreation.

"At first, those ideas seemed utopian. I would hear "This is America, we're going to have freeways, we're going to have cars, we're going to drive everywhere. Why should we walk places? We got past that sometime ago,'" recalls Calthorpe. "[But] in design, there are always fundamental shifts. There was [eventually] an increasing awareness about the environmental impact on our growth patterns and about the lack of a sense of community, of place, and of character. People started searching for alternatives and my work over the years has been to help create those alternatives."

In addition to teaching urban planning and architecture at several universities, Calthorpe has written numerous books that track a clear progression. In the early 1980s, with coauthor Van der Ryn, he wrote *Sustainable Communities,* which broadly outlined the environmental dimensions of urban design. In 1993, he introduced the concept of transit-oriented development and walkable communities in *The Next American Metropolis: Ecology, Community, and the American Dream;* and in 2001, he and coauthor William Fulton expanded this thinking of regional planning and urban revitalization with *The Regional City: Planning for the End of Sprawl.*

"Peter's combination of lightning-fast comprehension and speedy decisiveness gives him a confident, persuasive voice. He's not the only advocate for compact, mixed-use, walkable urbanism, but he's one of the most effective," says Doug Kelbaugh, dean of the A. Alfred Taubman College of Architecture and Urban Planning at the University of Michigan.

Calthorpe's understanding of the relationship between transportation and land use, combined with his expertise in regional-scale land planning and his passion for environmentalism, qualify him as "someone who has changed the world of land planning and development," Kelbaugh adds.

A map outlining the COMPAS regional visioning strategy for southern California. Calthorpe, along with partner John Fregonese, pioneered regional planning; their work includes the giant COMPAS plan. Their innovative community process and analytical tools have helped make planning at such a scale inclusive and implemental. *(Calthorpe Associates)*

SINCE RECEIVING THE NICHOLS PRIZE IN 2006

Peter Calthorpe has continued to foster awareness of environmental issues and to promote sustainable urban design practices. Through his work as a principal at Calthorpe Associates, he continues to publish important research and guidelines on sustainable community development.

In his book *Urbanism in the Age of Climate Change,* published in 2011, Calthorpe argues that sustainable urban development needs to play a key role in the fight to reduce carbon emissions. His book examines the cost of sprawl and the need for "green urbanism"—urbanism that uses more sustainable design principles and incorporates green technology and renewable energy. He writes, "Confronting climate change is a little like the war on drugs; you can go after a supplier—coal-fired power plants—or you can pursue the addicts—inefficient buildings and suburban sprawl. Both will be necessary."

Calthorpe's dedication to creating sustainable communities and alternatives to the suburban model for development continues to be recognized through the many accolades he has received. In 2012, Calthorpe received the Inaugural Atlas Award, "created to honor scientists, political leaders, authors, and many others for their leadership influencing Americans towards more caring and sustainable lives that could ultimately stabilize Earth's climate."

In 2013, he was named one of the Top 100 City Innovators Worldwide by UBM's Future Cities, an online community for innovation in global urbanization. In 2014, Calthorpe published a new book, *Transit Oriented Development in China: A Manual of Land-use and Transportation for Low Carbon Cities.* With his written contributions to the field of sustainable development, Calthorpe continues to leave his mark on the built environment, domestically and internationally. ■

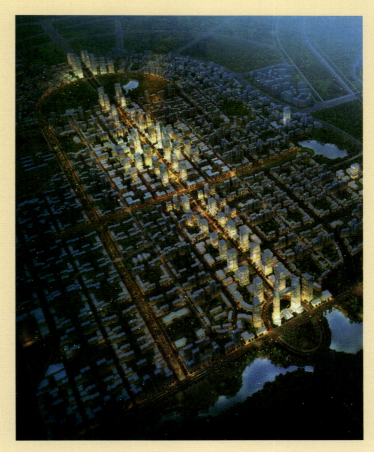

Chenggong New Town, Kunming, China. As one of the pioneers of transit-oriented development, Calthorpe has expanded on early theories in his 1993 book *The Next American Metropolis: Ecology, Community, and the American Dream* to include views on such projects outside the United States, with a particular emphasis on China. *(Calthorpe Associates)*

Calthorpe's influence is clear at the Denver mixed-use community of Stapleton, one of the nation's largest urban infill developments. When Cleveland-based Forest City Enterprises was selected by the city of Denver to redevelop the former Stapleton Airport site, the company was charged with implementing the city's plan to transform 4,700 acres of asphalt and concrete into an environmentally conscious, pedestrian-friendly community with ample green space. "Our challenge was to translate that concept into a physical plan, and what we had heard about Peter led us to him," says Ronald Ratner, president of Forest City Residential Group. (Forest City and its cochairman, Albert B. Ratner, were joint recipients of the 2005 Nichols Prize.)

According to Ratner, Calthorpe's expertise as a problem solver stems from his ability to think as a developer, an architect, an engineer, and a planner in order to fit all the pieces of a project together. "He has an amazing ability to deconstruct a problem, to get to the bottom of what people are saying. . . . Whether he is talking to traffic engineers or retailers, he extracts information and utilizes his principles to come up with a design solution. Peter is a craftsman at the top of his trade," Ratner says.

"Urban design," contends Calthorpe, "involves a nuanced set of tradeoffs. It involves a balance of design, economics, politics, and the marketplace; they are all integrated."

"Those who plan the way cities should develop are often unsung but vital to the process. He is at the forefront of a significant movement in redefining how urban areas should work."

JEREMY NEWSUM • 2006 JURY MEMBER

Calthorpe has an unusually keen understanding of both the micro and the macro aspects of urban design, and can easily switch from one to the other, notes jury member Leinberger. "He looks at the entire place-making process with a holistic view that what you build fundamentally affects the region, the country, the entire economy. . . . He understands that it is the environment and the people in that environment that count," Leinberger explains. "He wants to know what the market is thinking, the political context, the desires of the landowners—he is capable of taking in a great amount of data and focusing it on a design solution."

In *The Regional City,* Calthorpe and Fulton explain how regional-scale planning and design can integrate urban revitalization and suburban renewal into a coherent vision of metropolitan growth. Calthorpe has developed a regional visioning process that involves collecting an assortment of demographic, economic, and environmental data about the region, along with ideas from a broad cross section of stakeholders about future growth patterns. The data and the input from residents are combined into various scenarios, each of which reflects different choices for both governments and citizens. The public is then asked to choose the scenario it believes represents the best growth path for its region.

One of many gathering places in Stapleton's town center. When Forest City Enterprises was selected by the city of Denver to redevelop the former Stapleton Airport site, the company turned to Calthorpe for assistance with the design. *(Forest City Stapleton)*

Calthorpe recently conducted regional visioning workshops in some communities along the Gulf Coast, including New Orleans, which is still struggling to rebuild and bring back residents one year after Hurricane Katrina's destruction. Attendees "were willing to look at the whole picture of how the place should be rebuilt, and it was great to see people rise to that," Calthorpe says. "People tend to make the right decisions when they think long term and on a large scale. They sometimes make the wrong decisions when they think piecemeal. I help people reach their own decisions; it's a healthy interaction," he explains.

Perhaps one of the most widely acknowledged regional visioning successes is Envision Utah (a 2002 ULI Award for Excellence winner). The plan resulted from the Envision Utah Public/Private Partnership, formed in 1997 to guide the development of a high-quality growth strategy to protect Utah's environment, economic strength, and quality of life for future generations. The organization enlisted Calthorpe and his partner John Fregonese to "help us optimize opportunities for the region and come up with a vision," says Robert Grow, senior counsel at the law firm of O'Melveny & Myers LLP in Salt Lake City and the founding member of the Envision Utah partnership.

"When you are going about your daily routine, you are experiencing a set of places, and Peter knows how to create places to make that routine more enjoyable. And he has the capacity to see the big picture. Unless you understand the environment at a grand scale, you cannot design scenarios to pose choices the public will understand," Grow says. Calthorpe's ability to build consensus among people with diverse interests was a key factor behind Envision Utah's broad acceptance, he notes.

NEW URBANISMS

"There Are Many New Urbanisms"

Throughout the 1980s—a period Peter Calthorpe describes as "bleak" in terms of environmental awareness and prudent development—he remained determined to change the haphazard, poorly planned growth of American's communities. This spurred him to cofound the Congress for New Urbanism (CNU) in 1993, along with Andrés Duany and Elizabeth Plater-Zyberk, both principals at Duany Plater-Zyberk & Company in Miami; Elizabeth Moule and Stefanos Polyzoides, both principals at Moule & Polyzoides in Pasadena; and Daniel Solomon, director of Solomon E.T.C., a WRT company in San Francisco.

CNU advocates public policies and development practices that support more livable communities. Its advocacy is based on the belief that neighborhoods should be diverse in use and population; communities should be designed for the pedestrian and for public transit as well as the car; cities and towns should be shaped by physically defined and universally accessible public spaces and community institutions; and urban places should be framed by architecture and landscape design that celebrate local history, climate, ecology, and building practice.

The organization has a set of principles that apply to the design and development of all levels of community—such as the region, the city, and the block. The principles are not limited to American cities: CNU's charter is provided in Spanish, French, Dutch, Chinese, and Swedish, reflecting its global membership.

"If I were to summarize new urbanism, it would be very simple. New urbanism involves communities that are diverse and integrated, in terms of who is there and what is there. It takes in a full range of people of all colors and backgrounds—higher income, lower income, young, old, families, singles, the broadest range possible. It includes shops, schools, housing, parks, businesses, all the uses, all mixed together, all walkable. You cannot have good urbanism without that kind of diversity and walkability," Calthorpe emphasizes.

Calthrope is quick to explain that CNU's principles are guides, not mandates, leaving plenty of room for flexibility to meet the specific needs of a particular community. "There are many new urbanisms. The typical critique of new urbanism is based on a Seaside [a well-known new urbanist community] stereotype, not the movement's true range in scale, location, or approach. There are new urbanists who practice only infill, while some focus on new neighborhoods, and some are adamant about design standards and codes. And there are those like myself who do a bit of each and are much looser. The vitality of CNU comes from the fact that it is a diverse group of people who have differences of opinion and emphasis, but who share a common set of principles.

"There are examples of new urbanism as inner-city infill, as affordable housing, as transit-oriented development, and as a greenfield new town. No two projects are alike. There is no rubber stamp for all of them . . . there are examples of every single principle in the charter that have been consummated. Not all principles are used in one project, but you try to achieve as much as possible in any one circumstance."

Says 2006 ULI J.C. Nichols Prize jury chair A. Eugene Kohn: "Peter's views allow for individuality in that not every community is the same. His ideas about community growth allow it to take place according to what is natural for the area, keeping in mind environmental and transportation issues."

Calthorpe's ability to mold CNU's principles into a plan appropriate for both a development site and the surrounding region has been clearly evident to Peter McMahon, president of Kennecott Land in Salt Lake City. When he decided to hire Calthorpe to design the layout of the 4,200-acre Daybreak community, some in the company were skeptical that the new urbanist would craft a plan distinctive of Utah. "I told him, 'Daybreak has to have a Utah look and feel. If people come here and think it looks like something in Seattle, I am going to be really annoyed,'" McMahon recalls.

There was no need to worry. In a process similar to that for Envision Utah, Calthorpe worked with Kennecott to arrange a series of public meetings to determine what area residents wanted in that new community. With their input, he delivered a plan, that, while introducing features new to Utah such as alleys, narrower streets, and roundabouts, still "definitely respects" the character of the Salt

Calthorpe was hired by Kennecott Land to design Daybreak in Salt Lake City. "Urban design involves a balance of design, economics, politics, and the marketplace," he says. *(Kennecott Land)*

Lake Valley region in terms of architectural style, McMahon notes. "What he has done at Daybreak is working for our marketplace."

According to Calthorpe, the premise behind CNU can be attributed to J.C. Nichols's desire to build for permanence. "The new urbanism movement began with the model [similar to Country Club Plaza and the adjacent pedestrian-friendly residential neighborhood] and the life work of J.C. Nichols. He understood that a community was about integrating a full range of activities with housing, shops, schools, parks, and clubs. He understood the importance of streetscape. He wanted to build a community that would last for generations, and be socially and environmentally sustainable," Calthorpe says. CNU President John Norquist views Calthorpe's selection as the 2006 Nichols Prize laureate as a key recognition of new urbanism principles. "We want our ideas shared, and if they take firm hold, then our work will be done," he says. ■

Daybreak Community Center. "I told him [Calthorpe], 'Daybreak has to have a Utah look and feel,'" says Peter McMahon, president of Daybreak development company Kennecott Land. *(Kennecott Land)*

Following his work on Envision Utah, Calthorpe was hired by Kennecott Land of Salt Lake City to design a plan for more than 90,000 acres it owns, much of it in Salt Lake County. The plan includes designing the first development in the massive landholding, Daybreak, which will cover 4,200 acres. Like Stapleton, Daybreak will offer full-scale variety in housing choices and a mix of uses, and it will be heavily oriented toward pedestrian and transit use.

"Peter has strong opinions, but he understands that a developer has to be successful," says Kennecott Land President Peter McMahon. "We have pushed back on some of his ideas if we don't feel they are right, and he always works with us to get a good outcome."

"If you look at things regionally," says Calthorpe, "you can solve some of the problems at the scale of individual buildings or cities that seem intractable." Urban design—whether at the neighborhood or regional level—is about collaboration, he adds. "Everything I do is built on the shoulders of other people and is built on huge collaborations. My idea about design is to be as inclusive as possible, get as many ideas as possible on the table, and steal the best ones."

According to Jonathan F.P. Rose, president of Jonathan Rose Companies in Katonah, New York, Calthorpe "knows how to use things he has already done and apply them to new projects. This serves him well, because he is always looking for something he has not done before."

Rose has been Calthorpe's client since 1984—the two have worked together on several projects, including a live/work community with artist studios in Santa Fe and a "green" urban infill housing development in Denver. Rose also has a personal relationship with Calthorpe—he is married to Calthorpe's sister. "Peter and I do disagree on some things," says Rose, "and he loves a good discussion. If you engage him, he will dig in and engage back."

His brother-in-law, says Rose, "taught me how to really see cities and urban spaces. 'He said, when you walk in a city, don't look at the sidewalks. Look up, not down. Look at the buildings, look at the people, look at what's around you.'"

When Calthorpe looks at cities, he does not see grand designs, but evolving organisms that need room to grow and change. It's clear that the opportunity to be part of that growth keeps him motivated. "I want to bring back a sense of humility to how we shape our communities," he says. "I think people are desperate for a sense of community and place. When generic places are created, people are left with unconscious needs and wants—needs that can only be satisfied with more coherent communities. I think constantly about how to bring that about. You can be ideological about things, but if you cannot figure out a way to make them happen, all you're doing, at best, is putting words on a page."

2007

SIR STUART LIPTON

The Place Maker

Originally published in October 2007

It is summer, on a warm, partly sunny workday in London. Out at Stockley Park, a 400-acre business campus with a public park and public sports facilities near Heathrow Airport, employees are taking a break for lunch. Some are trickling toward the clubhouse and heart of the project to pick up takeout from the cafés. Some head down to sit next to the lake, with its sculptures of synchronized swimmers, each with one leg perched high in the air.

The fitness center is gearing up for the lunchtime crowd, and midday joggers head down the various landscaped paths. At a hilltop hole of the park's golf course, golfers take in a panoramic view stretching from Wembley Stadium to Windsor Castle. The setting offers a bucolic backdrop for the park's 2 million square feet of office space, occupied by more than two dozen companies involved primarily in technology and telecommunications.

Two hours later, at Chiswick Park, a 33-acre business park only 15 minutes from central London, workers are lingering outside over a late lunch. Chiswick, designed as a mid-urban place rather than a traditional business park, will, when completed, contain 2 million square feet of office space. It is home to many of London's media- and entertainment-related firms, including CBS News and the Discovery Channel, whose offices are located in the park's striking glass buildings designed by world-renowned architect Lord Richard Rogers.

On this day, a couple of people who work at Chiswick are returning hybrid bicycles loaned from the park's management office, called the Thoughtful Centre. A row of acoustic guitars is lined up against the center's wall, available to employees who feel like strumming during their free time. A young man dangles his foot in the stream running from a waterfall near one end of the park. In a few hours, there is likely to be a game of volleyball, soccer, or basketball on the multisport public space. As was the case at Stockley, the fitness center at Chiswick is a busy place.

Later, the close of the business day is nearing at the 29-acre Broadgate financial complex in downtown London. The center contains 4.5 million square feet of office, retail,

"Public space should be simple in concept, and perhaps complex in delivery and variety, so it can be used by different people in different ways. As a developer, if people are enjoying your project, you have fulfilled at least part of your obligation to society."

SIR STUART LIPTON • 2007 NICHOLS LAUREATE

A visit by Queen Elizabeth II (shown with Lipton) marked the completion of Broadgate in December 1991.

and open space. Women, in business suits and barefooted, are playing a game of croquet in one of the development's three public squares. People are starting to mill about an open-air pub. Another common area, used as an ice rink during the winter, has been converted to a putting green in anticipation of the coming British Open; golf legend Jack Nicklaus is expected to drop by later in the week. Around the corner, tourists are photographing themselves at the *Rush Hour* sculpture, which depicts workers heading between work and home. There are so many works of art throughout the complex—among them, *Bellerophon Taming Pegasus*, *Fulcrum*, *Leaping Hare on Crescent and Bell*, and *Broadgate Venus*—that a booklet has been published to identify them.

Stockley, Chiswick, and Broadgate could hardly be more different from one another in architecture, layout, and the types of companies operating in each. The common feature shared by these three major employment centers is ample, thoughtfully designed public space. These developments were built not just to serve as places to work but as places to enjoy. Places to relax, to meet old friends, and to make new ones. Places that appeal to workers and visitors with bold art and modern architecture.

This is precisely what Sir Stuart Lipton, the 2007 winner of the ULI J.C. Nichols Prize for Visionaries in Urban Development, had in mind when he developed all three centers. He understood long ago that the way people use space between individual buildings can be an energizer, providing an element of appeal that ultimately produces a greater return on the overall venture.

"When we think about spaces, we think about memory, warmth, and friendship—all that we naturally enjoy, all that will linger in our minds," explains Lipton, deputy chairman of Chelsfield Partners in London. "Everyone should be able to enjoy public space. It should be simple in concept and perhaps complex in delivery and in variety, so it can be used by different people in different ways. . . . [As a developer], if people are enjoying your project, you have fulfilled at least part of your obligation to society."

Lipton views making places as honoring the city, drawing on city building methods used not just by previous generations, but by previous civilizations. "One of the responsibilities of developers is that we must remember that cities should be a series of places.... The greatest places are those that generate civic pride. These are the places where people feel comfortable and safe, where they are allowed to exercise their civic persona and rights. We must respect the history [of a place] so that when people walk into it, it is reminiscent, it has memory, it has character," he says.

"When people feel they fit in, that they belong in a place, something magical happens. We know that when people feel safe, they are active, and they are better off mentally and physically. We know that kids behave differently in spaces that are well maintained. We know that crime is reduced in areas that are properly designed. The quality of space can really impact the way society behaves.... The power of space must be such that it has an influence on one's daily life."

Lipton, 65, is widely considered one of London's most visionary, creative, and committed developers. He began reshaping London's landscape in 1983, when he founded Stanhope Properties LC. Under his guidance, the Stanhope team developed, either on its own or in partnership with others, more than 50 office buildings providing more than 20 million square feet of commercial space in central London and the London environs. He is well known for shunning the predictable, preferring architecture, design, and amenities that surprise, delight, and soothe.

"It is fantastic fun being in real estate. It is emotional; it is every piece of humanity you can think of," he says. "If you understand what people like, you can provide the right development with the right services. There is a slight art form in this. It is providing something [people] like, but haven't thought of yet. You have to be a little inventive."

Jeremy Newsum of Grosvenor Estate in London points to Lipton's ability to successfully blend his passion for modernism with the architecture of an old city. "Building in London has always been a process of new development fitting in with the old. Having a view about what is there before creating something new is part of Lipton's makeup. He believes his work must improve the environment, help it adapt and evolve, meet the changing world around it, and be prepared to change again in the future," Newsum says. "As a result, the standard of architecture and development in London has continued to go up over the past 20 years, and it [the rising standard] is all feeding off his view that we can do better, that we can create something to be proud of."

Lipton is described by many as having an uncanny ability to see potential in sites that have interested few other developers. For instance, Stockley Park is on a former landfill; site preparation required the removal of 141 million cubic feet of garbage buried as deep as 40 feet underground. Chiswick Park occupies the former seedy site of an abandoned bus depot. Broadgate sits on a formerly derelict area that included the seldom-used Broad Street rail station; and the Liverpool Street station, next to Broadgate, was in dire need of a makeover.

Each set of obstacles left Lipton undaunted. "So often, the piece of development that is the problem becomes the opportunity," he says. Indeed, all of Lipton's projects—

SINCE RECEIVING THE NICHOLS PRIZE IN 2007

Sir Stuart Lipton has continued to create lasting impressions on London's landscape through place making and innovative human-centric public spaces. Speaking of his experiences in developing challenging projects with multiple elements articulated through urban open spaces such as Stockely Park, Chiswick Park, and Broadgate in the City of London, Lipton states, "When we think about spaces, we think about memory, warmth, friendship—all that we naturally enjoy, all that will linger in our minds. . . . Everyone should be able to enjoy public space. It should be simple in concept and perhaps complex in delivery and in variety, so it can be used by different people in different ways."

This is a guiding principle that Lipton has maintained in his projects since stepping down from CABE. At Chelsfield Partners LLP, where he rejoined former business partner Elliott Bernerd, among other initiatives he worked on the redevelopment of Camden, with a heavy focus on community creation. In 2013, Lipton left his position at Chelsfield to create a new property development company with Peter Rogers. Rogers was the former construction director at Lipton's famous Broadgate project. Aiming to be at the cutting edge of design and construction complexity, the new firm, called Lipton Rogers, has taken on projects such as the Silvertown, a 50-acre, 7 million-square-foot mixed-use project in East London.

Elizabeth House, another development project, in Waterloo, a 29-story, 1.4 million-square-foot mixed-use project started construction in 2013 and is expected to be complete in 2016. Through the Silvertown project, Lipton found, "With such strong support from the local community and stakeholders, we will continue to gather feedback and ensure that it is taken into consideration. We look forward to feedback on the more developed plans which will clearly demonstrate how local people have influenced our proposals."

Another recent Lipton Rogers project is an apartment complex in Kensington, London, designed by Rem Koolhass. Surrounding the former Commonwealth Institute building, the apartment building features a complex hyperbolic paraboloid copper roof and will be renovated for a new Design Museum. ∎

There were plans to demolish the old Commonwealth Institute building, but Lipton was among the vocal advocates for preserving the structure. He embraced the challenge of keeping the main element of the original building and creating an adjacent project that is just as daring as the original 1962 structure. *(Charlotte Gilhooly)*

ranging from the Ludgate development, to the Treasury Building, which houses the United Kingdom's finance ministry—could be characterized as, at a minimum, challenging.

Lipton readily labels himself as a risk taker. "One of my risks in life is being on the edge. If you are not on the edge, you are not really living life," he says. "Development does require a certain amount of madness. As you go near the edge, you know the task is extraordinary, but you know the benefit is extraordinary too. In development and design, it is easy to go for the lowest common denominator. You make the most money by not taking risks and by building boring buildings. Those of us who do take risks have scars on our body and spouses who think we are crazy, but at the same time we have enormous satisfaction in knowing that our projects are playing their part [in creating a thriving city]."

Of all Lipton's developments, Broadgate is perhaps the one most often cited as demonstrating his ability to conceive and execute a vision. In 1985, when British Prime Minister Margaret Thatcher launched construction work at the development, she referred to it as the "largest single development in the city since the rebuilding of London after the Great Fire of 1666." She returned one year later to inaugurate the first buildings.

"Places like Broadgate really created the infrastructure needed for London to flourish as a financial center," says ULI Nichols jury member Witold Rybczynski, Martin and Margy Meyerson Professor of Urbanism at the University of Pennsylvania in Philadelphia. "After that, all sorts of other developments came along, turning London into a much more cosmopolitan city, a more prosperous city, one with qualities that seem obvious today, but which were not preordained by any means. Stuart Lipton had a vision of what London might be."

The vision Lipton had for Broadgate alone is sufficient evidence of his place-making skills, notes his longtime friend and business associate Paul Morrell, former senior partner with Davis Langdon, a construction and quantity surveying consultancy firm in London.

"He anticipated how the [financial center of the] city would move, and he knew the importance of building around transport hubs. This combination of office buildings, public rail, and related uses has given new life to the [Broadgate] area," Morrell says. "Not many people think on a scale large enough to think about place. They think 'What can I do inside this line?' Stuart has always looked outside the line and on to context. He thinks with his guts, and he's got the cleverest guts I've ever seen. He has an instinct for making places." Morrell has worked on several projects with Lipton over the years and served with him when Lipton chaired the Commission for Architecture and the Built Environment (CABE) from 1999 to 2004. (CABE is a U.K. nonprofit advocacy group created by the British government to advise the government—in its capacity of representing public users of the built environment—on effectively working with the design, planning, and development industry.) "Anyone can preside over something that would have happened anyway," Morrell notes. "That is not Stuart. He's always looking to change things." In addition to place making, Morrell credits Lipton with being a trailblazer in two other areas: in considering the needs of building users as part of the development process and in bringing together the architectural and development communities.

Stockley Park, a 400-acre business campus near Heathrow Airport, is built on the site of a former landfill. Site preparation required removal of 141 million cubic feet of garbage.

Before Broadgate was built, "we [the development community] were not building the right kind of office buildings. We just rolled out a cookie-cutter solution. Stuart started doing extensive market research to find out what people wanted, and how it would impact business," Morrell recalls. "He did that not just for altruistic reasons—he looked at it as 'If you make something work better, you can sell it for more.' He was the first to consider building in that way."

The inclusion of top-quality architects—at the time highly unusual in commercial development—was part of Lipton's earliest concepts of building a better product, Morrell continues. "When he started, our best architects would not work with developers, because developers were seen as building block merchants. Stuart breached that gap; he connected the worlds of design and commerce, sometimes by banging their heads together." Lipton's commitment to raising the bar for building quality with excellent architecture eventually evolved into CABE building guidelines; as a result, many developers now recognize high-quality architecture as an economic imperative, Morrell notes. "CABE has very successfully shown developers how to respond to context."

"What Stuart has done is to create environments that make places more memorable over time. His work is not just about development, but about civic contribution."

BONNIE FISHER • 2007 JURY MEMBER

Lipton credits Peter Rees, longtime city planning officer for the City of London, with encouraging architects to design buildings that have a civic purpose and a functional purpose, as well as the broader purpose of improving the overall quality of life in London. "By encouraging good architecture as well as good spaces, Peter has been able to get developers to compete with each other. That is a marvelous consequence of great design." Says Rees: "Most developers understand the need to put up buildings, and some . . . understand the need to create spaces, but few understand how to make a new place. It has to do with good-quality architecture, fine landscaping, and activity. And, at the end of the day, it is people that make places. Lipton understands that process."

For decades, Lipton has worked with Richard Rogers, chairman of Rogers Stirk Harbour + Partners in London, and with his brother, Stanhope executive Peter Rogers, a former partner of Lipton's and the construction director at Broadgate when it was being built. "Stuart is probably the most creative developer I have ever worked with. He understands the difference between merely building, and the implications of building on society. That is quite unusual, not just for developers, but for people," says Richard Rogers.

One of the keys to Lipton's enduring success is his unwavering belief that architecture must relate to urban context, Rogers observes. "People notice the spaces between the

"We Must Build Better, Safer, Simpler, and Bolder"

Stuart Lipton has participated in both World Cities Forums hosted by ULI; he cochaired the first, held in 2005 in London, and was a panelist at the second, held in April 2007 in Shanghai. Whereas the first event focused on building sustainable cities for the 21st century, the second examined sustainability through the lens of emerging cities, particularly those in fast-growing Asia. While attendees at the 2007 forum were awed by the magnitude of investment and development in Shanghai, concerns were expressed about whether the projects being built will withstand the test of time and change. Lipton shares his thoughts on the rapid growth in Shanghai and other cities in China and about sustainability in general:

"Shanghai is a very complex issue. You could compare what's going on in China with the postindustrial evolution of Western society. In the United Kingdom, for instance, in the 1850s, 1860s, and 1870s, we had a huge explosion of [growth in] cities, and we built new railroad stations, new factories, new ports, and warehouses. This displaced thousands of people; it broke all the rules. So, when I think of Shanghai, I think a lot of people are asking too much, because they are asking the people of Shanghai to skip a century [of postindustrial change].

"What I see in China is a democracy emerging; I see a society changing from war to peace. What I do know is once you start getting a taste for a new quality of life, once you get that bug, everyone wants it. . . . We can only hope that their [the Chinese] way of life will change.

"If we want to talk seriously about sustainability, leadership is required from our [political] leaders. Cities are much more sustainable [development environments] than countryside. So you could argue that the Chinese, having facilitated development in cities, are leaders. . . . Here we are talking about Shanghai's lack of knowledge, and who are we to criticize when we have not solved our own problems? Don't we need to give the Chinese help by showing the way forward? They are building new sustainable cities like Dongtan, which in concept are way ahead of anything in the United States or the United Kingdom. So, how can we demonstrate a new holistic version of sustainability?

"How can we provide a lifestyle that reflects the state of the 21st century that we live in? It is quite clear that to make our cities more sustainable, we must build better, safer, simpler, and bolder. . . . When we talk about issues related to sustainability, we should be designing environments where people can walk to work, where they have comfort in spaces, where everything becomes integrated, where, through lifestyle expectations, we are less dependent on cars. . . . The key to the future is development that is truly mixed-use. . . . It's not just an issue of high density. What we need is less dispersal and more community." ■

buildings as much as they do the buildings themselves, and Stuart understands that. He is a sophisticated urban planner."

Regarding the impact of architecture, Lipton recalls the words of his late friend Peter Foggo, whose team at Arup Associates in London designed Broadgate: "'You can't have every building being a firework.' So, you decide if you want the space to be your firework or the buildings." Ultimately, because of the draw of the space, the firework at Lipton's developments is the power of the workers, shoppers, and tourists bringing the place to life. "My firework is people," he says. "Open space is the one element that gives staying power to a development," says ULI Nichols jury member Bonnie Fisher, principal and director of landscape design at the ROMA Design Group in San Francisco. "What Stuart has done, more than many other developers, is to create environments that make places more memorable over time. He has demonstrated how they [open spaces] become the framework, the heart of all the activities in the buildings surrounding them. His work is not just about development, but about civic contribution."

Lipton's interest in the civic extends far beyond his own work. As a board member of the Royal Opera House, he was instrumental in the facility's regeneration and rebuilding, says Royal Opera House chair Dame Judith Mayhew. She recounts how, under Lipton's guidance, the redevelopment not only expanded the flexibility of the existing space, but also added tremendous public space through the renovation of the adjacent historic Floral Hall. It was, she says, a labor of love for Lipton. "Stuart made the opera house what it is today. . . . He has a passion for the arts, he has a passion for culture. [In working on the project], he was able to use his building, architectural, and regeneration skills alongside his passion for opera and ballet. I think it's probably the best renovation project in the whole of Europe. . . . It has lifted the whole area."

Mayhew concedes that the project's complexity made Lipton's vision difficult to execute. "But, as usual, Stuart produced it in the end." Lipton's many contributions to London's built environment have been triggered "not from a sudden leap of blood to the head on his part, but from deep convictions about the nature of the building and the nature of the design," says longtime friend Lord Dennis Stevenson, chairman of the HBOS plc financial institution headquartered in Edinburgh, Scotland. "The point about Stuart is that he is unbelievably decent, passionate, and emotional. With him, you get what you see. He is an absolutely nonpetty person who wears his strengths and weaknesses on both sleeves."

In describing the lasting influence of Lipton's work, Stevenson continues, "Stuart would say he has not done anything particularly radical, that he has simply met a market need. . . . He does not think of himself as a trendsetter. He's just being Stuart. If being a trendsetter means someone who bravely does something ahead of the pack, Stuart's got quite a track record of that."

Opposite:

Top left: Former British Prime Minister Margaret Thatcher (shown with Lipton) described Broadgate as the "largest single development in the city since the rebuilding of London after the Great Fire of 1666."

Top right: The *Rush Hour* sculpture at Broadgate is among the most photographed pieces of art in London.

Bottom: The striking glass buildings at the 33-acre Chiswick Park were designed by Richard Rogers. The park, designed as a mid-urban place rather than a traditional business park, attracts tenants with the motto: "Enjoy work."

2008

F. BARTON HARVEY III AND ENTERPRISE COMMUNITY PARTNERS

The Myth Breaker

Originally published in October 2008

Opposite: Galen Terrace is the first rehabilitated property in the District of Columbia to meet all the green criteria under the Enterprise Green Communities® initiative. The 83-unit project involved rehabilitating an existing Section 8 housing community of three apartment buildings on two parcels in the Anacostia neighborhood.

On weekday mornings, Whatcoat Street in Baltimore's Sandtown neighborhood is a quiet place; most of the residents of the neat brick townhouses have left for work. However, on a sunny day in August, Sandtown homeowner Deborah Hammond had a few hours to spare before heading to her job at a local medical institution. She smiled as construction workers completed the installation of an awning over her patio. It was the latest of several improvements—including new wood floors—she has made to her home since purchasing in Sandtown.

"I love it here, and I am never leaving," she says. "All the neighbors here look out for each other. We are a very close community. There is no crime. The troublemakers know to stay away from this block. I would not want to live anywhere else. This is my home, and I don't have to worry about losing it. I did not buy more than I could afford."

Hammond's 1,200-square-foot townhouse, which she bought for about $60,000 in 1995, is one of 300 built during the early phase of a comprehensive neighborhood rehabilitation conceived in the late 1980s by legendary community builder James Rouse, the late cofounder and chairman of what was then called the Enterprise Foundation, based in Columbia, Maryland.

The nationally acclaimed affordable housing investment and development organization, since renamed Enterprise Community Partners, has continued to revive the area, working with other organizations either to rehabilitate or build nearly 300 additional units. Although nearby streets still have plenty of boarded-up buildings, it is clear that the neighborhood as a whole is in the throes of promising transition.

Sandtown, the first comprehensive neighborhood transformation project tackled by Enterprise after Rouse formed the organization in 1982, is a "fabulous symbol" of what the organization has accomplished in cities across the United States, says Enterprise Homes President Chickie Grayson. "As you drive around cities all over the country, you see a lot of 'for sale' signs popping up like weeds. There is not one 'for sale' sign here in Sandtown. People really value what they have here and they want to hold on to it. They intend to keep their homes for generations to come."

"The people in our communities are rooted. When people have a stake in their community, they want to see better things happen. They look out for their neighbors; they try to make sure crime is diminished. It's a tremendous positive for the whole community."

F. BARTON HARVEY III • 2008 NICHOLS LAUREATE

Left: A block in Baltimore's Sandtown neighborhood before Enterprise started redevelopment in the area.

Right: Housing units in Sandtown redeveloped by Enterprise. Sandtown, one of the first rehabilitation projects tackled by Enterprise after James Rouse formed the organization in 1982, is a "fabulous symbol" of what the organization has accomplished in cities across the United States, says Enterprise Homes president Chickie Grayson.

A highly regarded leader in the funding and production of affordable housing, Enterprise now has operations in 17 metropolitan regions across the United States working with local community development corporations, other nonprofit organizations, developers, investors, and elected officials to build affordable housing that is integrated into the greater community. The organization has grown exponentially over the past two decades. Enterprise has raised more than $9 billion in private capital for the production of nearly 250,000 homes, the majority of which are targeted to people making no more than 60 percent of the median income for their communities.

Enterprise's impressive expansion is due, in no small part, to the leadership of F. Barton Harvey III. Harvey joined Enterprise in 1984, serving as chairman and chief executive officer of Enterprise Community Partners from 1994 to 2007 and as chairman of the board of Enterprise Community Investment from 1993 until his retirement this past March. During Harvey's time at the helm, Enterprise's impact grew from $200 million annually to help provide 5,000 affordable homes per year to more than $1 billion raised and invested annually to create more than 20,000 units per year.

Harvey, 59, attributes the success of Enterprise to committed and able colleagues and an endless demand for affordable housing. "Enterprise has been so successful in good and bad economic times because of the large need in this country for affordable housing—obviously for those with very low incomes, but also for working-class people who have been priced out of the housing market," he says. The demand, notes Harvey, steadily increased over the years and shows no signs of diminishing, because of the lack of new supply and the persistent nationwide loss of low- to moderate-income units that either have been torn down or have been converted to higher-end, market-rate housing. "It is a huge issue for hardworking people and those with special needs," Harvey says.

The extraordinary strides Enterprise has made in filling in the affordable housing gap has earned both Harvey and the organization the 2008 ULI J.C. Nichols Prize for

Visionaries in Urban Development. The $100,000 annual prize, which honors ULI founder and legendary Kansas City developer J.C. Nichols, recognizes an individual or both an individual and organization demonstrating a longstanding commitment responsible development.

"Enterprise represents the more altruistic aspect of the development community," says Nichols Prize jury chair Jeremy Newsum, group chief executive of Grosvenor in London. "What it brings [to the land use industry] is an understanding of the less-advantaged society, and the need for affordable housing and expertise in how to create it. In every city of the world, there are people doing great things that are unsung and unheard. The fact that Enterprise has been able to do this type of work on this scale is what impressed the jury."

Jury member Paul Schell, former mayor of Seattle and strategic adviser for NBBJ in Seattle, praises Enterprise's success in galvanizing and working with local nonprofit organizations, which he views as critical in helping communities thrive. "As a former mayor, I have always been struck by how much the nonprofit sector does in our cities. [The nonprofit sector] takes on the issues that are real challenges for mayors. Enterprise has fostered a tremendous involvement by community-based organizations."

Indeed, Enterprise's work makes for a very positive housing story in the midst of a stubbornly persistent national housing downturn and subprime home mortgage calamity. Whereas the vast majority of units developed and financed by Enterprise are rental units, the owner-occupied homes that have been financed by or developed through the organization tend to have low turnover rates and low mortgage foreclosure rates. This is due primarily to comprehensive homeownership preparation and counseling that prospective buyers must complete.

One example: in 2007, the Federal Reserve Bank of Dallas analyzed the city of Dallas's mortgage assistance program (MAP), a downpayment and closing cost assistance program for below-median-income buyers that is administered by Enterprise Community Partners. The Fed found the foreclosure rate for homes purchased through MAP between 1997 and 2005 to be 2.4 percent, far below the 6.7 percent rate for all subprime conventional loans in Texas during approximately the same period. "MAP households are not as likely to purchase homes that are too expensive in relation to income. As a consequence, the MAP default and foreclosure rates are much lower than those for subprime loans—the most likely alternative for low-income households—in Texas," the analysis states.

Whether rental or owner-occupied, Harvey points to the community-wide benefits generated by providing safe, fit, affordable housing in pleasant living environments. "The people in our communities are rooted," he says. "When people have a stake in the community, they want to see better things happen. They fight for better schools; they look out for their neighbors; they try to make sure crime is diminished. It's a tremendous positive for the whole community."

The opportunity to provide an environment that instills community pride, and ultimately, long-term sustainability, is exactly what Harvey says kept him at Enterprise for 24 years— far longer than the six months he initially planned to serve while on a sabbatical from a

Wall Street investment banking career. Rouse, he notes, had convinced him within one year to switch gears permanently, to "become an investment banker for the poor instead of the rich."

Harvey was not immediately hooked, but it didn't take long. At their first meeting, Rouse enthusiastically described his purpose for creating Enterprise—to see that all low-income people in the United States have the opportunity for fit and affordable housing and to move up and out of poverty into the mainstream of American life within a generation. Although Rouse was a highly acclaimed developer of marketplaces such as Baltimore's Inner Harbor and the planned community of Columbia, Maryland, he emphasized that what he sought to accomplish through Enterprise would be perhaps his most important work.

"I left thinking Jim was crazy," Harvey recalls. "I thought, 'You and what army are going to do this? How are you going to singlehandedly change the country?' But he had achieved so much in his life, that I thought, 'Well, I can do this for six months. And [during those months] as I watched him work, I realized there can't be anything better than helping people help themselves," recalls Harvey.

"I had a remarkable set of experiences meeting people who were positive grassroots leaders, who had seen enough of the bad and wanted to change their neighborhoods for

SINCE RECEIVING THE NICHOLS PRIZE IN 2008

Bart Harvey and Enterprise Community Partners have continued their unwavering support to accomplish an equitable built environment.

The year 2008 saw a housing crisis that devastated so many families, led to millions of foreclosures, and wreaked havoc on the housing finance industry, making it tremendously difficult to find investors able to invest in affordable housing at a critical juncture. But as Enterprise has always done, the organization rose to the challenge and remained steadfast in its goal of ensuring that every person in this country has the chance to live in an affordable home in a thriving community.

That year, Enterprise led the Save America's Neighborhoods campaign that spurred the creation of the $4 billion federal Neighborhood Stabilization Program, aimed to help communities at risk of foreclosure. Also in 2008, Enterprise celebrated a remarkable milestone—a total of $10 billion in community investments since its establishment in 1982.

Bart Harvey's retirement one year earlier had already sparked leadership changes at Enterprise, with Doris Koo managing the organization from 2007 through 2010. Terri Ludwig—a 25-year veteran of the industry—was appointed as president and chief executive officer of Enterprise Community Partners in 2011. Charles Werhane took the helm of Enterprise Community Investment in 2009, following Jeffrey Donahue's retirement.

In 2012, Enterprise's highly regarded cofounder and wife of the late James "Jim" Rouse, Patty Rouse, died at age 85. "We are forever indebted to Patty, our visionary cofounder, for her unwavering commitment and the groundbreaking legacy she has left the affordable housing and community development industry," said Ludwig in a statement released following Patty Rouse's death.

April 26, 2014, marked what would have been the 100th birthday of Jim Rouse, who remains an ongoing inspiration for the affordable housing industry. Hailed by *Time* magazine as "the man who made cities fun again," Rouse famously revitalized urban landscapes by building "festival marketplaces" such as South

the good. I was enthralled with them, with the hope and possibility they presented, and the ability to use what I'd learned on Wall Street to connect money and resources with people who had the nerve and daring to believe there was a better life and a better way for these communities. The next six months became 24 years and I never looked back."

Over time, it became evident that Harvey was just as committed to advancing Enterprise's mission as Rouse, says Rouse's wife, Patricia Rouse, co-founder, vice president, and secretary of Enterprise Community Partners. "With all the other things Bart could have been doing, we both were very impressed that he was spending time with us at Enterprise. He was innovative and willing to take on things that people generally did not want to take on. Without Bart, Jim wouldn't have been able to accomplish what he did."

Doris Koo, president and chief executive officer of Enterprise Community Partners, recalls working with the organization 25 years ago, while serving as a community organizer in New York City. She was aiming to rehabilitate two burned-out buildings into 59 affordable units, a project she realized was relatively small, but one she felt was well worth pursuing. "Jim and Bart convinced me that there is nothing more important and fulfilling than to follow your heart, to be grounded in communities, and to trust in the wisdom and instincts of the struggling families whose lives are not connected to you in any way other than by

Bart Harvey (right) with James Rouse during Enterprise's early days. "As I watched him [Rouse] work, I realized there can't be anything better than helping people help themselves," Harvey says.

Street Seaport in New York City and Faneuil Hall in Boston. But he considered Enterprise "by far the most important work" of his life.

Harvey remains devoted to Enterprise's cause and continues to serve as informal counsel to the organization. "Bart remains a visionary and visible leader, lending his voice and advocating for affordable housing by demonstrating that it is both a sound financial and social investment in our communities," said Ludwig. Harvey is a director of Fannie Mae under its conservatorship and remains active in a number of local and national nonprofit organizations. He is on the board of the Calvert Foundation; a trustee of Calvert School in Baltimore, Maryland; a member of the investment committee for the Blue Mood Fund; and a member of the Garrison Institute's advisory council. He is actively involved in various ULI awards juries, recently serving as jury chair for the Gerald D. Hines Student Urban Design Competition. Harvey is also a former member of the advisory board for ULI's Terwilliger Center for Housing.

Enterprise's Green Communities® initiative, a program launched under Harvey's leadership, boasts continued success. Since the program's inception in 2004, the program has created and rehabilitated more than 38,000 green and affordable homes, with more than $2.89 billion invested.

"We continue to be inspired by Bart's legacy and have taken tremendous steps forward in advancing his philosophy that housing is a platform for opportunity," said Ludwig. "Enterprise's family of companies has grown significantly since 2008, expanding our geographic reach, product offerings and level of investment in affordable housing and community development nationwide. With the help and generosity of our partners and supporters, we invested $2.5 billion in communities, financed more than 16,800 homes and supported 24,500 construction-related jobs in 2013 alone. Each affordable home we have helped build or preserve represents a real person or family—and a platform to the opportunity for a more rewarding life." ∎

the fact that their fate could be forever changed by your work," she says. "There are a lot of cynics who say, 'Poverty is too big for us to attack.' I've learned that poverty can be alleviated building by building, block by block. But at the end of the day, we have to scale up our solutions." To accomplish more, Koo cites three goals to which Enterprise is unwaveringly committed: to provide practical solutions to the nation's toughest challenges in housing; to continue seeking resources and capital to aid in overcoming those challenges; and to make significant, positive changes in housing policy that result in the best housing practices becoming commonly applied practices.

The numerous local partnerships Enterprise has forged with community nonprofit organizations has "cleared a pathway for community builders" to make an extraordinary difference, Koo says. "Bart's biggest legacy is that he gave a voice to a generation of community builders, allowing them to believe in themselves because he believed in them. Bart is happiest when he's among the families and children who have had a chance to move into these communities. He has truly humanized the community development world."

"The nonprofit sector takes on the issues that are the real challenges for mayors. Enterprise has fostered a tremendous involvement by community-based organizations."

PAUL SCHELL • 2008 JURY MEMBER

"Bart has the same gift Jim had, which is the gift of meeting and gathering people who can get the job done," says Jeffrey Donahue, president of Enterprise Community Investment. "We have a wonderful development company, to be sure. But of the $1 billion that Enterprise invests each year, over $900 million goes toward helping someone else build housing. [In that regard,] we're a service organization, and if you are a service organization, it's the quality of the people you have that really makes a difference. You work here because you really like the work and you want to work with the other people here. Bart was the salesman for that [enthusiasm] for 24 years, 24 hours a day. He was always fired up."

Notes Carol Galante, chief executive officer of Bridge Housing Corporation in San Francisco: "Enterprise has always been interested in the community from a holistic standpoint, in that it's not just about the housing, it's also about the safety and the educational institutions—everything that makes a community work. As a community investor, Enterprise seeks to ensure that the social components are doing equally as well as the real estate components. They [the staff members] understand that social investment keeps communities sustainable."

Richard Baron, cofounder, chairman, and chief executive officer of McCormack Baron and Salazar in St. Louis, Missouri, was selected as the 2004 ULI J.C. Nichols Prize laureate in recognition of the great strides he has made as a private sector developer of affordable housing. Enterprise has invested in some of the McCormack

Baron and Salazar projects; and Baron has a longstanding relationship with Harvey. He participated in an advisory group of real estate industry leaders that Harvey convened over a period of years to vet ideas and discuss new directions for Enterprise.

"Bart started out as a missionary, in terms of his commitment (to nonprofit development of affordable housing). But over time, he understood that there are private sector approaches [to building affordable housing] that work," Baron notes. Mixed-income housing, which incorporates below-market-rate with market-rate housing, was one approach embraced by Harvey during his "metamorphosis," Baron says. "He grew with the program, and became much more of an advocate for rebuilding whole neighborhoods as opposed to just providing affordable housing. Bart was the perfect person to take Enterprise to the next level and expand its programs."

One expansion has been in the area of workforce housing, a category of housing distinguished from affordable housing in that it is targeted to people who do not qualify for any government housing assistance programs, yet fall far short of being able to afford housing in the communities where they work. J. Ronald Terwilliger, former ULI chairman and current Enterprise Community Partners trustee, provided a substantial boost to this initiative for Enterprise in 2007, when he donated $5 million to the organization for the development of workforce housing. Terwilliger, chairman and chief executive officer of Atlanta-based Trammell Crow Residential, also donated $5 million to ULI for the creation of the ULI Terwilliger Center for Workforce Housing, which seeks to work with local stakeholders to increase the supply of workforce housing in markets nationwide.

Terwilliger, who is also a member of the Enterprise real estate advisory group formed by Harvey, explains that his decision to make the donation to Enterprise was guided by Harvey's intelligence, skill, commitment, and financial acumen. "I was impressed with his ability to leverage equity capital and donations to raise substantial funding," Terwilliger says. "I liked Enterprise's business model. I felt that Bart could make $5 million go a long way, and that the organization would be a good steward of the funds."

Another expansion of the organization is Enterprise's Green Communities® initiative, launched four years ago under Harvey's leadership. It represents an unprecedented commitment to bring the economic and environmental benefits of sustainable development to low-income communities. To date, Enterprise has committed over $570 million to cities nationwide to develop more than 12,500 green and affordable homes. The initiative was honored earlier this year as one of nine global winners of the 2008 Urban Land Institute/ Financial Times Sustainable Cities awards, which recognize ongoing programs that exhibit new ideas and perspectives for future practices in sustainable land use.

As Harvey contemplated the green concept, he sought advice from Jonathan F.P. Rose, president of Jonathan Rose Companies LLC in New York City. Rose convinced Harvey that environmentally conscious affordable housing could be built in a cost-effective manner. He also persuaded him that providing healthier living environments by "going green" fit perfectly with Enterprise's goal of investing in people. "In a brief time, Bart not only got that, but he imagined something that was unimaginable, which was how to make all affordable housing green," Rose says.

The Oleson Woods apartments is an Enterprise Green Communities® development just outside Tigard, Oregon, a fast-growing suburb of Portland. The project consists of 32 newly built townhouses and flats in six residential buildings in the Metzger-Progress neighborhood.

Harvey announces a Green Communities® development in San Francisco. Since Enterprise started the program four years ago, the organization has committed over $570 million to provide more than 12,500 green and affordable homes across the nation.

High Point, a Green Communities® development in Seattle, Washington, consists of 320 newly built homeownership units and 459 rental units in West Seattle. Some 344 of the rental units are syndicated with low-income housing tax credits.

Harvey started "changing the pieces of the system," which led to guidelines from Enterprise for green construction of affordable housing that were designed for use by community development corporations. In addition, a growing number of states started offering tax incentives for green and affordable development. The swelling support for green and affordable housing as a result of Enterprise's involvement leads Rose to believe that it will be sooner rather than later when all new housing will be green. "Bart has a real knack for being able to say there is something there, and then turning what's there into a big reality," Rose says.

The Green Communities® initiative includes a partnership with the Washington, D.C.–based U.S. Green Building Council (USGBC), which years ago started a certification system for green development. Both organizations "share values that really focus on the people that live and work in the buildings," says Rick Fedrizzi, president, chief executive officer, and founding chairman of the council. He credits Harvey with helping USGBC concentrate its expertise in an area of real estate that had been largely overlooked in the green building movement. "For instance, when you start looking at the ability of a single mom to be able to pay a lower monthly utility bill and more of that money can go for food or into her child's education—to improve that family's way of life—then you realize the agenda is solid," Fedrizzi says.

Harvey, Fedrizzi adds, has also emphasized that housing that is located close to transportation and jobs is part of the greening factor. "Bart's leadership really helped take the thinking on this from the building level to the community level."

Harvey says he was shocked at how quickly local public officials clamored for the money allocated for the program's first phase; the $500 million allotted for grants and technical assistance was gone within half the time scheduled for its use. "The rest of the country is way ahead of the federal government on this. There is an understanding that we need to build in a different way," Harvey explains. "Out of this initiative came a sense that we're still just touching the surface; that the environmental community and the building community need to come together in a whole new way to look at land use. I see Enterprise as being one step in a whole building movement that will change the way we build in the future."

Harvey has long been recognized as a strong advocate on Capitol Hill for the affordable housing industry, pushing for federal housing policy changes designed to spur development of low- and moderate-income housing. He and Rouse are credited with spearheading the creation of the Low-Income Housing Tax Credit, a federal tax credit created under the Tax Reform Act of 1986 that provides incentives for contributions of private equity in the development of affordable rental housing.

The tax credit provides funding for the development costs of low-income rental housing by allowing an investor to take a federal tax credit equal to a percentage of the cost incurred for development of the low-income units in a rental housing project. Development capital is raised by syndicating the credit to an investor or, more commonly, a group of investors. The program is administered at the state level with each state getting a fixed allocation of credits based on its population.

According to the U.S. Department of Housing and Urban Development, more than 1.3 million units were constructed using the tax credit through 2005. The current economic downturn has diminished demand for the credits, as investors such as financial institutions have incurred losses and have less income to shelter. Still, the tax credit has a history of being highly effective. "It has proved to be one of the single most important tools in producing low-income housing," Harvey notes.

Enterprise joined several other housing advocates to rally for key measures in the federal housing legislation enacted last summer to assist homeowners facing foreclosure and financial institutions stuck with bad loans and foreclosed properties, as well as to help communities in acquiring foreclosed homes and placing them back on the market. Among the key provisions: authorization of $300 billion in Federal Housing Administration loan guarantees for a voluntary program to help at-risk borrowers refinance with viable mortgages; and a $3.9 billion grant program for state and local governments to purchase foreclosed homes.

"I look at this housing legislation very positively, but I think it may be only the first step in stabilizing the housing market," Harvey says. "It's time to right the ship, for the government to intervene in a prudent way to keep people in housing."

Koo of Enterprise Community Partners points to a silver lining in the housing debacle—an increased national awareness of the importance of decent housing as a key contributor to community stability. "It's unfortunate that it's taken a housing crisis of this magnitude to highlight the significance of having a place that one can call home. But we will take this challenge and turn it into an opportunity to further strengthen neighborhoods to make sure they are not destabilized as a result of the financial crisis."

Although Harvey feels that Enterprise continues to fight an uphill battle in reducing the shortage of affordable housing, he looks back with pride on its accomplishments—not just in building units, but in changing perceptions.

"We've dispelled some myths about affordable housing," he says. "The first was that it is an uneconomical and financially risky investment and should be considered as a charitable write-off. Enterprise showed major financial institutions that this is a financially responsible investment. The second myth was that the housing we build will be trashed. The reality is that virtually all our housing is more valuable now than when it was first built. It's a community asset. The third myth was that all Americans ought to be homeowners. They shouldn't. There is a critical role for rental housing in this country, and there are certain families who are just not ready to be homeowners. I'm very proud of the role Enterprise has played in affordable rental housing.

"The final myth is that affordable housing destroys communities and destroys home values. We've proven time and time again that this is not the case. My greatest joy in being part of Enterprise has been to see a family who never thought they would be able to afford a home get into a home and feel that they have achieved permanence to their existence and a better future for their kids," he says. "If we can provide a platform that is more nourishing and which helps more people to succeed, then that translates into a more productive society."

2009

AMANDA M. BURDEN

Growing New York One Block at a Time

Originally published in October 2009

Opposite: On the site of an elevated railroad line built in the 1930s on the west side of Manhattan, a new landscape has emerged. The High Line is an elevated boardwalk with seating, plantings, and views of the Manhattan skyline and the Hudson River.

At midmorning on a clear day this past August, people were already strolling along the High Line, a new linear park in Manhattan. For first-time visitors, it's an experience as surprising as it is pleasant, because the High Line is anything but traditional urban parkland. The nearly two-mile-long park is built on an elevated, abandoned railway that stretches from the Meatpacking District to the West Side Rail Yards. Hovering between 20 and 30 feet above ground level, the public park provides a sense of detachment, but not total isolation, from the urban activity below.

The first half-mile portion (mainly in the Meatpacking District) of the park opened in June 2009. At the southernmost entry point, a new Whitney Museum of American Art is proposed. Further up, the recently renovated Standard Hotel straddles the park, its rooms overlooking the walkway. At the park's intersection with West 17th Street, rows of benches behind a plate-glass wall offer a perch from which to watch traffic zipping up Tenth Avenue. As the park nears the West Chelsea arts district, the "iceberg" building, designed by Frank Gehry and nicknamed for its distinctive shape, comes into view.

The park—part of the West Chelsea/High Line plan (one of the 2009 winners of the Urban Land Institute's Awards for Excellence: the Americas competition)—is positioned to offer views of both New York's west side and the Hudson waterfront. At one point, the Statue of Liberty is easily visible in the distance. The High Line mixes portions of the old weathered railroad tracks with lush landscaping, striking angular benches, and wooden chaise lounges. Meadow grass and a wide variety of wildflowers have been planted to mimic the greenery that spread over the railway as it sat unused for the past 30 years. Clearly, this is a space meant for taking in the city at a slower pace.

Amanda M. Burden, chair of the New York City Planning Commission and director of the New York Department of Planning, gazes down the walkway at the foliage, the people, and the architecture. Even though the High Line has yet to be completed, its early success—as evidenced by the multitudes of visitors so far—affirms a vision for the space that she has held steadfastly for the past decade.

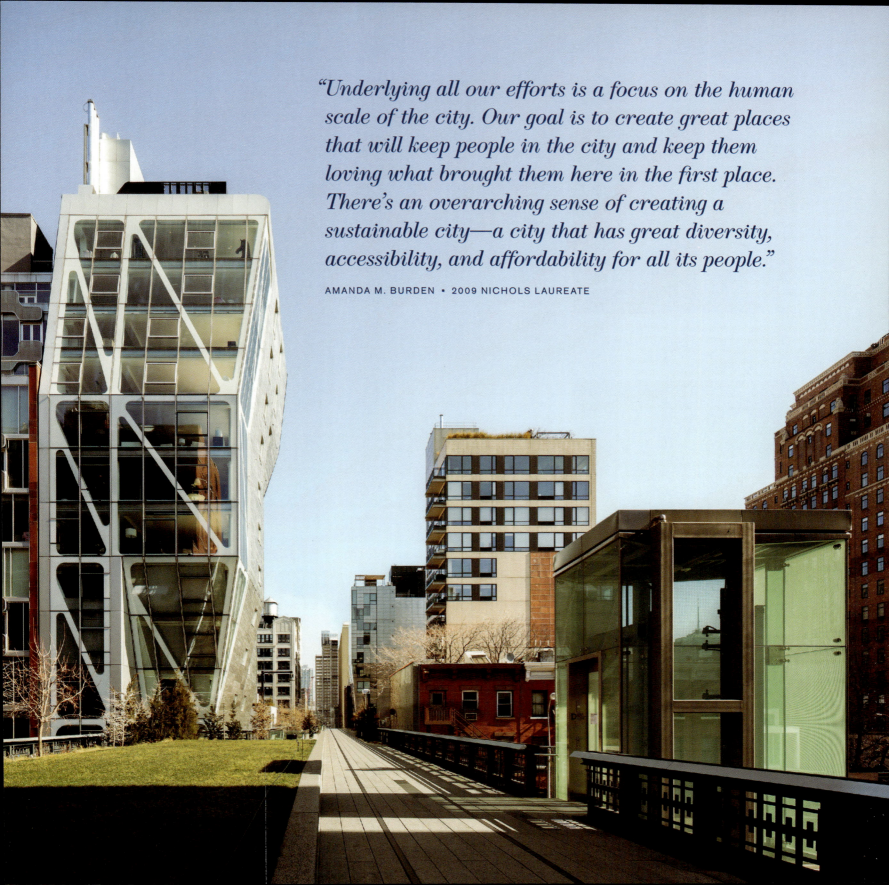

> *"Underlying all our efforts is a focus on the human scale of the city. Our goal is to create great places that will keep people in the city and keep them loving what brought them here in the first place. There's an overarching sense of creating a sustainable city—a city that has great diversity, accessibility, and affordability for all its people."*
>
> AMANDA M. BURDEN • 2009 NICHOLS LAUREATE

Burden describes the High Line as "a wild garden in the sky, a floating vantage point from which you can be both part of the city and apart from it."

Major urban planning initiatives underway in New York City include the transformation of the Fresh Kills landfill on Staten Island into parkland.

"Of all the projects I've worked on, the High Line is one of my favorites," says Burden. "It's a visually magical park, a wild garden in the sky, a floating vantage point from which you can be both part of the city and apart from it."

Burden points to the building designed by Gehry, to another by Jean Nouvel, and to still another by Audrey Matlock. In addition to being a key public amenity, the High Line has catalyzed more than 30 new private development projects along the adjoining areas. "Some of the world's most distinguished architects are clamoring to build here. None of those [development projects] would have happened if not for the High Line," she notes.

The High Line is but one of many ambitious redevelopment projects Burden has championed during her 19 years of service on the planning commission. Since 2002, the year Mayor Michael R. Bloomberg appointed her to serve as commission chair and planning department director, the department has updated decades-old zoning codes, and the commission has approved 100 large rezoning initiatives covering more than 8,000 blocks throughout New York's five boroughs, as well as thousands of smaller-scale private rezoning applications. To date, the rezonings have covered nearly one-fifth of the city's 322 square miles.

Major initiatives underway include master plans for the East River waterfront in lower Manhattan, downtown Brooklyn, Long Island City and Jamaica in Queens, as well as the city's largest plan—Hudson Yards—which will provide 24 million square feet of office space and more than 12,500 units of mixed-income housing. Projects on the to-do list: new housing, including affordable housing, for Greenpoint/Williamsburg in Brooklyn, east and central Harlem, and Port Morris in the Bronx, and the transformation of the Fresh Kills landfill on Staten Island into parkland.

With a population of nearly 8.4 million people who live in more than 188 neighborhoods in which more than 200 languages are spoken and with an average population density of 25,400 persons per square mile (the highest is 128,600 per square mile on Manhattan's upper east side), New York City presents, by any measure, a daunting planning challenge. Burden's approach to such a complex task is straightforward: to grow and transform the city one block at a time, in a way that respects the heritage and character of each neighborhood.

This means making multiple visits to each block considered for rezoning to talk with those who live and work there and to observe how they use public spaces.

"New York is a global city, but most importantly, it's a city of neighborhoods. The essence of good planning is to really understand the constraints and opportunities in each neighborhood and to build from the characteristic strengths found in each one," Burden explains. "Underlying all our efforts is a focus on the human scale of the city. An overriding goal is to create great places that will keep people in the city—keep them loving what brought them here in the first place. There's an overarching sense of creating a sustainable city—a city that has great diversity, accessibility, and affordability for all its people."

Mayor Bloomberg cites two qualities—long-term vision and an ability to engage people—that make Burden particularly effective as the city's top planner. "She doesn't look at zoning as just zoning. She looks at it as setting a plan for development for decades," he says. "She has great commitment and compassion and an ability to work with people. You can have the greatest ideas, but with zoning, you're always going to have some people in favor [of change] and some against. She has infinite patience to answer all the questions at town meetings. She goes out, she visits sites. All of that comes through, so that even if you disagree with her, it's hard not to have respect for her.

"In New York, we live as a mixture, not a mosaic. When you walk down the street, you'll get a tour of the world in one block. Amanda understands that. She is trying to create a future without destroying neighborhoods. We have to make sure that people can enjoy what's good about New York."

This firm dedication to improving the quality of life in New York—through more public space, more affordable housing, and a greener environment—has earned Burden the 2009 ULI J.C. Nichols Prize for Visionaries in Urban Development. The $100,000 annual prize, which honors ULI founder and legendary Kansas City, Missouri, developer J.C. Nichols, recognizes an individual whose career demonstrates a longtime commitment to the highest standards of responsible development.

> *"Amanda represents an aspect of implementing a vision that can often be lost in the public perception. . . . At the end of the day, everything relies on the execution."*
>
> JAMES M. DEFRANCIA • 2009 JURY CHAIR

The selection of Burden—the first city planner to be awarded the prize—is a celebration of those charged with bringing grand visions to fruition, says Nichols Prize jury chair James M. DeFrancia, president of Lowe Enterprises Community Development Inc. in Aspen, Colorado. "Amanda represents an aspect of implementing a vision that can often be lost in the public perception. When you implement, you have to have the whole vision, but you're also dealing with the nuts and bolts of making it happen. At the end of the day, everything relies on the execution."

Adds jury member Paul Schell, a former mayor of Seattle: "Mayors often get the credit for everything, but no mayor can be effective without having the right people on the front lines. Amanda is a wonderful example of somebody on the front lines who's getting things done."

An Intelligent City Plan

Ninety years ago, J.C. Nichols wrote, "an intelligent city plan thinks impartially for all parts of the city at the same time and does not forget the greater needs of tomorrow in the press of today." The citywide plan being implemented by Burden illustrates that Nichols's insights still hold true. The plan builds on the economic potential not just of Manhattan,

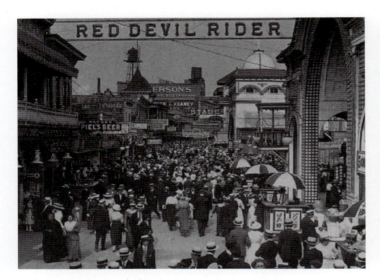

Coney Island in its heyday (left) and a rendering of its planned restoration (right). The long-struggling oceanfront amusement park will be revived through a comprehensive plan that will benefit the entire area with a year-round entertainment district, new housing, and neighborhood retail.

but of Brooklyn, Queens, the Bronx, and Staten Island. "New York has often been very Manhattan-centric, but we need to grow in each borough. We need to understand where we should grow, where we should recapture our waterfront, and what we should preserve," she explains.

The plan aims to channel the most growth around New York's transportation infrastructure and to channel it away from areas reliant on auto use. Because of the city's numerous transit options, it already has a lower carbon footprint related to vehicle use than other more auto-dependent cities. In some cases, "down zonings," which limit heights and density for new development, in lower-density suburbs are combined with "up zonings" along higher-density transit corridors.

A case in point: the Bedford-Stuyvesant neighborhood in Brooklyn, a neighborhood of restored brownstones, was rezoned in 2007 to keep out oversized development; and to counter this down zoning, the city is allowing higher-density apartment buildings to be erected over the retail space along the nearby bustling Fulton Street corridor. Under the city's inclusionary housing provisions, affordable units must be part of the housing if developers want to reach the maximum building height. "What we are doing is developing a framework for communities to grow, not to change. We are preserving what is best, what is cherished, and at the same time finding opportunities for new development," Burden says.

"Amanda has a real sense of how urban design and economic goals have to be aligned," says ULI trustee Robert C. Lieber, New York's deputy mayor for economic development. "The changes in the design and urban planning that we're putting in place today are changes that will last forever and will play out over decades as we move forward.

With the scarce land we have here, we're recycling a lot of what we have. Coming up with the appropriate uses [for land] in the future is a hallmark of what she brings to this role."

Lieber points to the recently approved redevelopment plan for Brooklyn's historic Coney Island as one of many examples of Burden's long-term view of how best to reshape New York. The long-struggling oceanfront amusement park will be revived through a comprehensive plan that will benefit the entire area with a year-round entertainment district, new housing, and neighborhood retail. "Amanda's vision is not what Coney Island is going to look like next summer, or in five years. It's the impact on the residents in ten, 20, or 30 years," he notes.

Long-range city planning will no doubt be one of the legacies of the Bloomberg administration, says Nichols Prize jury member Elizabeth Plater-Zyberk, founding partner of Duany Plater-Zyberk & Company in Miami. "Many cities, like New York, are dealing with issues of how to grow on land that has already been developed once," she says. "Decisions about what to preserve and what to develop are of critical importance. The plan the city of New York has been working with does precisely that—it outlines what to save, what's available for development to house increasing numbers of residents and encourage economic development, and how to better use land that over time has become underused."

SINCE RECEIVING THE NICHOLS PRIZE IN 2009

Amanda Burden has continued to expand her efforts to improve design excellence and community consensus building across the urban environment.

Burden donated the prize money to establish the ULI Urban Open Space Award to celebrate and promote urban open spaces that enrich and revitalize surrounding communities.

"It has been my life's work to celebrate the essence of city life and to create great public open spaces," Burden says.

Since its inception, the award has recognized projects across North America that showcase the critical qualities that these public open spaces offer to facilitate meaningful urban development. The winners include Campus Martius Park, Detroit; Citygarden, St. Louis; Railroad Park, Birmingham; The Parks and Waterfront at Southeast False Creek, Vancouver; and the Yards Park, Washington, D.C.

Burden was commissioner for the New York City Department of City Planning from 2002 to 2013, spearheading the largest planning effort in the city since 1961; initiating comprehensive rezoning plans for 124 neighborhoods—almost 40 percent of the city; and catalyzing significant new housing opportunities in diverse communities throughout New York City's five boroughs.

Shortly after the end of her tenure, she joined Bloomberg Associates as principal for urban planning. This philanthropic venture seeks to help city governments improve the quality of life of their citizens. Burden supports the consultancy work to improve urban environments by collaborating with cities on developing best practices, building consensus, and fostering key relationships, and to continue turning her dynamic vision into reality. ∎

Paley Park to Battery Park

Burden's interest in urban planning and design—particularly related to public spaces—was instilled in her by two major influences: her mentor, urbanologist William "Holly" Whyte, widely considered as the inspiration for the Project for Public Spaces, a nonprofit group in New York devoted to the creation of open spaces as community focal points, and her stepfather, CBS chief executive William S. Paley, who built Samuel Paley Park, a 4,200-square-foot pocket park on East 53rd Street in Manhattan. The park, named for Paley's father, has a water wall that buffers noise and offers a respite from the din of midtown.

Burden credits both Whyte and Paley with showing her the key contribution that public space makes in a city's overall success. "That [creating appealing public places] is really what drives me today. All the mammoth plans really come down to the granular approach of how a building meets the street, how a street feels, how you feel walking in the city and coming to public spaces that are inviting. Public space is why you stay in the city," she says.

Paying attention to the details of design is the difference between a successful public space and a failure, Burden notes. It's a lesson she experienced early in the design of Manhattan's Battery Park City. From 1983 to 1990, she served as vice president for planning and design of the Battery Park City Authority, overseeing the design of all open spaces, including the waterfront esplanade and 30 acres of parkland.

The area was bare—nothing but 90-plus acres of sand dredged from the site upon which the World Trade Center towers had been built. The authority decided to play up the appeal of public space to incentivize private sector interest in investing in and developing a full-scale community with housing, retail, and commercial uses. A small part of the esplanade was constructed to illustrate what was to come. "We built a mock-up of the seawall, railing, and a bench. When I sat down, the rail was right in front of my eyes, and I couldn't see anything," Burden recalls. "We redesigned it. We knew we could not get that wrong, because that rail would be running a mile and a half along the river. Getting it [the height] right made all the difference.

"Good design is about getting all the details right, it's about individual perception, the activation of the senses. If a space is successful, it can be pivotal in turning a place into a successful community."

Richard Kahan, former chairman and chief executive officer of Battery Park City, says that Burden's ability to think simultaneously about the largest and smallest components was integral to the project's success. "She has a rare combination of gifts—the ability to see the big picture, and a great capacity for focusing on details," explains Kahan, now president and founder of the Urban Assembly in New York City. "There are people with large visions who never see them implemented. And there are people who are focused on minutiae, but never have a larger vision. Amanda incorporates both in one person."

Kahan attributes Burden's insistence on strict building design guidelines in Battery Park City with triggering the application of tougher design standards throughout the city.

Opposite:

Top left: The waterfront in Battery Park City. "Good design is about getting all the details right, it's about individual perception, the activation of the senses," Burden says.

Top right: The Bedford-Stuyvesant neighborhood in Brooklyn, a neighborhood of restored brownstones, was rezoned to keep out oversized development.

Bottom: Burden "doesn't look at zoning as just zoning. She looks at it as setting a plan for development for decades," says New York City Mayor Michael Bloomberg (second from right).

"She has elevated, in a way that we have not seen in many years, the importance of high-quality building design and high-quality public space," he says.

Walking the City

During her years on the planning commission, Burden has gained a reputation not just for familiarizing herself with the city's blocks by covering them on foot, but for enlisting her colleagues, including former commission member Deborah C. Wright, in the task. In Burden's mind, there simply is no better way to understand the complexities of the city and make informed decisions about the implications of planning proposals, Wright explains. "Amanda is not just a planner or theorist. She's a walking practitioner of planning in the city," says Wright, president and chief executive officer of Carver Bancorp in New York City. "She loves designs that are inspiring, but she knows that the prettiest designs won't work unless the spaces are usable and truly appreciated by the individuals who live and work in them.

"You have to get on the street and understand what's different about south Bronx than Harlem or Fulton Street in Brooklyn or the middle of Williamsburg or Jamaica. She's put the time into knowing the differences between those neighborhoods. She's invested in the people who are there."

Wright points to Burden's commitment to reviving Harlem's 125th Street, on which the Apollo Theater is located. A few years ago, the two friends went to a show at the Apollo, and when it ended, they stepped out onto a dark, empty street. That experience, says Wright, etched in Burden's mind the need for a plan to energize the area, to draw more residents as well as visitors. "She got it, just like that," Wright says.

The proposal has multiple objectives: to preserve the scale of the historic corridor while maintaining its rich cultural heritage and providing substantial affordable housing. The rezoning was the first in the city to offer a density bonus in exchange for providing arts-related uses. Burden built consensus by working with an advisory committee composed of more than 100 Harlem business and local civic leaders, community board members, and elected officials.

"It [the redevelopment plan] is designed to support 125th Street, so that it can have the economic base it needs to thrive," Wright explains. "Amanda found a way to economically integrate the street, and now people of means will move there, given what has happened. But it's stayed true to its character, and it's accessible to everyone, no matter what their means."

"What we are doing there [on 125th Street]," Burden says, "is reclaiming and reinventing an iconic place in New York that was on the verge of losing its soul."

The *Zoning Handbook*

One of the most effective tools the department of planning uses to build community support for all its efforts is the *Zoning Handbook*. First issued in 1973, it has been updated to introduce new zoning concepts and zoning changes enacted in recent years. But more

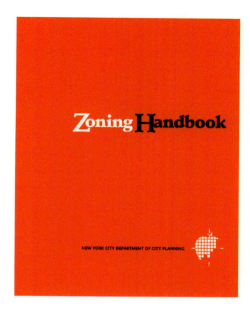

The updated version of the city's *Zoning Handbook* presents information in a way that is easily understood and visualized, using pictures and drawings to illustrate and differentiate various zoning designations. The handbook's demystification of zoning has eased the approval process for many projects, Burden says.

important, the updated version presents the information in a way that is easily understood and visualized, using pictures and drawings to illustrate and differentiate various zoning designations. Without question, the handbook's demystification of zoning has eased the approval process for many projects, Burden says. "It explains just what people can expect and helps them be better advocates for their neighborhoods. Now, we regularly see community advocates bringing in dog-eared copies to community meetings."

The book is illustrative of Burden's strong belief in community engagement in the planning process. "I spend an enormous amount of time working directly with communities to help them understand our proposals and to understand their concerns. You have to invest the time to have their trust and be able to have a plan that meets their needs.

"In New York, we have changed the way the planning process functions. It's a collaborative approach, incorporating community desires into a citywide policy. I could not do this job without listening to the people, hearing them talk about their hopes, their dreams, what they want, and what they don't want. Our grand plans mean nothing unless they are embraced by the community."

2010

An Urban Artist

Originally published in October 2010

(City of Chicago)

Opposite: Mayor Daley joins members of the Pilsen community to celebrate the new playground at Jefferson Playlot Park. *(City of Chicago)*

A cobalt-blue sky serves as the backdrop for this stunning summer Chicago day, comfortable and clear. In this city known for its architectural wonders, seemingly everyone finds his or her way outside.

Near the north branch of the Chicago River, a mother pushes her infant in a baby swing at a triangle-shaped playground in a pocket park. On the Northwest Side, high school students create a garden to beautify their solar-powered school. Elderly folks walk to the new shopping center that has a bank and a grocery store on the West Side. Further east, a family leaves the Field Museum, strolling past flowers and trees on the lakefront Museum Campus as they head to a picnic outside the Adler Planetarium. And just east of Michigan Avenue, tourists search to find themselves in the giant, polished silver "bean," officially known as *Cloud Gate*, in Millennium Park.

How and where these people are spending this beautiful afternoon illustrate Mayor Richard M. Daley's imprint on Chicago. Daley, who recently announced that he will not seek reelection in 2011, will be leaving the people of Chicago a legacy of successful community building that stretches over his 21 years in office. He has transformed this Rustbelt city into a revitalized international metropolis, bringing together the built and natural environments to make the city more sustainable, livable, and lively.

"A lot of people here in Chicago think that Mayor Daley is really this century's [city planner Daniel] Burnham, and in many respects he is," says Donna LaPietra, president of Millennium Park Inc.

Daley's ability to bring his intertwining priorities to fruition has earned him the Urban Land Institute's prestigious ULI J.C. Nichols Prize for Visionaries in Urban Development for 2010, making him only the second mayor so honored in the award's 11-year history. The $100,000 annual prize, which honors ULI founder and legendary Kansas City, Missouri, developer J.C. Nichols, recognizes an individual whose career demonstrates a longtime commitment to the highest standards of responsible development.

"Mayor Daley does it, and nobody does it better," says Nichols Prize jury chair James M. DeFrancia, president of Lowe Enterprises Community Development Inc. in Aspen,

Colorado. In selecting Daley, the jury considered the broad template of changes fostered during his time in office. "That included everything from green roofs to transportation systems to improving entire neighborhoods. [It was] the whole rainbow of all those activities," DeFrancia says. "We talk about cities where we want to live, work, and play, and that's what he's created in Chicago," adds jury member Deborah Ratner Salzberg, president of Forest City Washington in Washington, D.C.

"Nature Can Coexist with the City"

Among the mayors Daley respects are New York City's Michael R. Bloomberg, Boston's Thomas M. Menino, and Philadelphia's Michael A. Nutter. "Mayors understand they need common sense, and they have to work hard to get what they want accomplished," he says. Unlike many politicians, Daley shies away from attention, preferring not to take credit for the city's many accomplishments. He is quick to cite city planners, artists, the people, even Lake Michigan as the reasons Chicago is so successful.

Washington Square Park in Chicago. "To me, nature can coexist with the city," Daley says. *(City of Chicago)*

"We're really fortunate. We're one of the few cities [that] ever kept the waterfront," he says. "And just think—the Burnham Plan protected it. When you go all the way from Indiana, all the way almost to Evanston, it's all open space. That is very important. And to me, nature can coexist with the city."

Born April 24, 1942, the fourth of seven children, Daley entered a family involved in politics. Home was a modest house in the South Side's Bridgeport neighborhood, a place where residents are defined by their Roman Catholic Church parish, and most everyone loves the Chicago White Sox. In 1989, after years of serving as state senator and county prosecutor, Daley followed the footsteps of his late father, Richard J. Daley, into Chicago's City Hall.

A quick study, Daley is known for reading everything, cutting it out of magazines and newspapers, and passing it on. Daley takes the Burnham adage "Make no little plans" to heart. Compatriots say he knows every corner of the city, every park, every elevated train stop, and every parking lot. Even as a passenger in a car, he is on the clock.

"He sees everything. He takes notes constantly. He's always looking," says LaPietra. "I can't imagine that even his sleep time isn't involved with envisioning how the city could be better, how it could grow. He doesn't just dream the idea: he actually understands how you get it done."

Unlike other Rustbelt cities in the past 20 years, Chicago has grown—in population, diversity, jobs, and income. Crime is down, making residents more comfortable to visit and enjoy new attractions, parks, and neighborhood amenities.

"He has a kind of do-it-and-fix-it attitude, which is rare in political circles," says jury member Elizabeth Plater-Zyberk, principal of Duany Plater-Zyberk & Company LLC in Miami.

Daley knows the desire of Chicagoans for recreation matches their intense work ethic. On his watch, the city developed 200 acres of parks and green space, plus planted thousands of trees along miles of major roadways. But one green space perhaps more than any other forever changed the city's image. Millennium Park, which opened in 2004, serves as Daley's gift to the future. The 24.5-acre park wedged between Michigan Avenue and the lake stands as Chicago's most ambitious public/private undertaking, at a cost of $475 million, according to the *Chicago Tribune*. Millennium Park is now the city's top tourist destination for both tourists and residents and has become a model of public/private partnership, with more than $200 million contributed by private donors.

Previously, old railroad tracks and an empty parking lot pockmarked the southern end of historic Grant Park, scarring the face of showpiece Michigan Avenue. But in this space, the mayor envisioned a free park for families of every economic class, every ethnicity. He saw a palette for young artists to leave their mark—something more important, Daley claims, than a mayor's impact.

"We in politics think that what we do has an impact. But an artist, what they do in life—that lives forever," Daley says. "I think artists can define a city much better than anyone else."

Millennium Park is now the world's largest rooftop, sitting above active railroad tracks, and is an economic development engine for the downtown area, further attracting businesses and enriching the city's image as the home of major works of public art. The Jay Pritzker Pavilion, anchored by a silver band shell created by architect Frank Gehry, draws listeners to free concerts by world-class musicians. Steps away, the Lurie Garden offers visitors a respite, surrounding them with butterfly weed, purple prairie clover, and rusty foxglove. Anish Kapoor's popular *Cloud Gate* sculpture vies with the Hancock Building and the Willis Tower for the title of Chicago icon. The park's buildings meet tough environmental standards.

"He could see what it would be. I mean, those are concepts that only artists can understand. Daley took in the ideas," says Chicago journalist and documentarian Bill Kurtis. "Is the art in making it happen?"

Holiday shoppers crowd Michigan Avenue.
(City of Chicago)

An Unrelenting Focus on Sustainability

Chicago has been a leader in the environmental movement. Daley started to act in this arena shortly after becoming mayor two decades ago, proceeding in ways that many other cities are just beginning to appreciate and emulate today. The beautification of Chicago stems from Daley's focus on sustainability. "While many cities just set a broad goal, Chicago has gone to work at it in a very different way—almost with a mobilization of the entire city. They [city officials] had hundreds of meetings with neighborhood leaders, saying, 'Here's where we see the problems. How do you relate to it?'" says jury member Neal Peirce, chairman of the Citistates Group and a nationally syndicated columnist for the Washington Post Writers Group in Washington, D.C.

Today, Daley's focus on creating a sustainable environment remains fixed, even as other cities pull back in this tough economy.

"If you invest in an environmental manner, it saves money in the long run. It saves your health. It saves the air. It saves everything around you," Daley says.

He wants Chicago to be America's greenest city. Every new building in Chicago must strive for Leadership in Energy and Environmental Design (LEED) certification for energy efficiency and conservation. In late 2009, 88 Chicago buildings claimed LEED certification—more than in any other U.S. city.

> *"He has a 'do-it-and-fix-it' attitude, which is rare in political circles."*
>
> ELIZABETH PLATER-ZYBERK • 2010 JURY MEMBER

Daley's approach to achieving this goal has been to lead by example. In 2001, he ordered a 20,300-square-foot green rooftop for City Hall, aiming to lower energy costs and help mitigate the urban heat-island effect. At least 400 other Chicago buildings followed suit. An avid cyclist, Daley has been a bike commuter, encouraging Chicago's workers to leave their cars at home.

"You can't put all the cars on the highway. It's impossible," he says. "Public transportation should have a higher priority. It has to be clean, safe, on time, and friendly. If you miss any parts of that, then people don't like to use it."

The Ripple Effect in One Neighborhood

In Englewood, on the city's West Side, a bus stops at the corner of West 69th Street, just as the Reverend Willard Payton walks out the door at the New Birth Church of God. Vacant lots sit across the roadway; boarded up homes line the side streets. Payton is focused on the building across Laflin Street—Wheeler House, an independent living facility for seniors. Inside the well-kept four-story brick building, he finds two residents sitting in the sunlit atrium with comfortable furniture. Opened in 2003, Wheeler House provides studio and one-bedroom apartments to 89 seniors with incomes of less than $30,000 a year.

Englewood's aging population needed a place to live with dignity. "It's one of the visions, long term, of our church to provide services for the seniors of the congregation and of the community. We had senior members in our congregation who had outlived their children," Payton says.

Wheeler House was conceived in response to the neighborhood's longtime shortage of housing affordable to seniors. Once the church purchased the neighboring lot, public and private partners provided funding for the development, including a loan from a local bank, federal funds provided through the city of Chicago, and additional funding from the state and low-income housing tax credits obtained through Enterprise Community Investment.

Wheeler House created a ripple effect in Englewood. New businesses include a Salvation Army center, a library, a full-service bank—the neighborhood's first in decades—and a seven-acre shopping center on Ashland Avenue anchored by a Jewel grocery store.

"Wheeler House is an example of Mayor Daley's Chicago," says Jen Buxtin, director of asset management for Enterprise Community Investment. "The mayor recognizes that affordable-housing residents are not some subset of society. They're our neighbors, our relatives, our coworkers, and they deserve a place to age with dignity in place in their neighborhood."

During Daley's tenure, more than 170,000 units of affordable housing have been built, upgraded, or maintained throughout Chicago with investments of more than $4 billion in local, federal, and private funds. In his view, adequate affordable housing is one of the core components of a thriving city—one just as critical to long-term viability as high-quality education and highly efficient public services.

Daley also believes that the city's overall progress is perhaps best measured by what is accomplished in the most challenged areas of the city. "Each community is connected to another community. Each block is connected to another block," he says.

Opposite:

Top: Members of the Daley family (wife Maggie, front; Elizabeth Daley, and Patrick Daley, back) listen as the mayor announces his decision at a September 7 news conference not to seek reelection in 2011. *(City of Chicago)*

Bottom right: Cloud Gate, a popular destination for visitors to the city's 24.5-acre Millennium Park. Opened in 2004, the park has become a model of public/private partnership, with more than $200 million contributed by private donors. *(City of Chicago)*

Bottom left: In 2001, Daley had a 20,300-square-foot green roof planted on top of City Hall in an effort to lower energy costs and help mitigate the urban heat-island effect. At least 400 other Chicago buildings followed suit. *(City of Chicago)*

Left: Wheeler House, an independent living facility on Chicago's West Side, was conceived in response to the Englewood neighborhood's longtime shortage of housing affordable to seniors. *(City of Chicago)*

Right: The Urban Prep Academy in Chicago, the nation's first all-boy public charter high school composed entirely of African American students, achieved a 100 percent college acceptance rate for its first graduating class in 2010. "These students represent the 'I will' spirit of Chicago," Daley says. *(City of Chicago)*

"A City for the People"

Nearly 15 miles north of Wheeler House, Northside College Prep High School principal Barry Rodgers watches sophomores rush to hug each other at their orientation. Here, 1,100 of the city's best and brightest teens attend a school rated tops in the state for every year of its ten-year existence.

Northside Prep is not a private school. It is a Chicago public school, and, as is the case at the city's other eight merit-based high schools, its student roster represents a range of economic and ethnic groups. Two years before Daley's election, U.S. Education Secretary William Bennett declared Chicago's public schools "the worst in the nation." Once in office, the Daley administration took over the school system, overhauling everything from the basic curriculum to the actual structures. The Chicago Public School (CPS) system invested more than $5 billion in building improvements, and 41 new schools have been constructed—the first being Northside Prep. Today, CPS test scores are at an all-time high, and dropout rates are sinking. "Fast forward 20 years and we're now a model urban public school system," Rodgers says. In fact, CPS now claims three of Illinois's top five schools, and *U.S. News & World Report* ranks Northside Prep 37th in the nation.

"The most important aspect of livability is the quality of education that you give to a family," Daley says. "If you offer good early childhood education, and good elementary and high schools, you'll keep families in the city."

At Northside Prep, all of Daley's priorities—education, neighborhoods, sustainability, and beautification—come together on one campus. Northside Prep students, concerned about their school's energy use, initiated a plan to install six solar panels and found funding via public agencies and private companies.

Outside, four boys move mulch onto the new Joy Garden, filled with tomatoes and cornflowers and environmentally friendly materials such as porous concrete. Their interest in landscaping grew from a summer jobs program Daley developed. But as summer ends, this becomes an organic movement as these students continue working with volunteers to create a Joy Garden club.

"This has become part of the culture. This has become part of the expectation of what they believe should happen in a city," Rodgers says.

"Not only are our students going to have a better life in terms of their income and job opportunities, but they're going to be the difference makers—the positive change agents in society," he adds. "They're going to be people that innovate with new green technologies. They're going to be the people who are the CEOs—but they're the responsible CEOs of companies, people that give back to their community . . . the people that make it the fabric of a successful society."

While many point to Millennium Park or the cities LEED-certified buildings as Daley's lasting imprint, Rodgers instead points to his students' academic records, as well as their work to make the environment sustainable. "This is the mayor's legacy. He's passing this on for our future generation," he says.

By virtually any measurement, Daley's commitment has made Chicago a more accessible and more enjoyable city for all its residents. However, he is quick to point out that lasting success depends on goals shared and pursued by the public and private sectors. "You have to make sure the amenities are there—the schools, the parks, the open space, the cleanliness . . . and that the business community and the people in government are working together," he says.

Adds LaPietra, "If [Daley] is any one thing, he is an artist. He is an urban artist—today's most contemporary, most forward-looking artist in terms of how you envision a livable city, a city for the people."

SINCE RECEIVING THE NICHOLS PRIZE IN 2010

Richard Daley has continued to effect change in his home city of Chicago. With 22 years as mayor of Chicago and more than 40 years of public service, Daley has left his mark on the city for years to come. Since his retirement from public service in 2011, Daley has worked in a number of positions to continue helping cities grow responsibly.

Seeking other ways besides public office to aid his city, Daley joined the international law firm Katten Muchin Rosenman LLP only weeks after his term as mayor ended. There he negotiated Chicago's long-term leases for its parking meters and other leases in the Chicago Skyway and city parking garages.

In addition to improving the built environment of Chicago, Daley found ways to influence cities around the world. In 2011, the University of Chicago appointed Daley distinguished senior fellow to the Harris School of Public Policy. As a five-year appointed senior fellow, he is responsible for coordinating a guest lecture series with influential policy makers from around the world to provide insight into critical urban policy challenges. Daley also was appointed managing principle of Tur Partners LLC, an investment firm that partners with leaders and innovators to drive growth in global urban environments.

Daley was also named the senior adviser to JPMorgan Chase, where he chairs the Global Cities Initiative, a joint project of JPMorgan and the Brookings Institution, to help cities more effectively compete in the global economy. Daley was also appointed cochair of President Obama's 100,000 Strong initiative, a program that aims to increase the number and diversity of American students studying in China to foster a stronger people-to-people tie between that country and the United States.

Through various opportunities, whether coordinating lectures with influential policy makers or chairing a new global cities initiative, Daley continuously finds new and creative ways to influence the built environment. ■

2011

HIS HIGHNESS THE AGA KHAN

A Humanitarian Vision

In 2011, the Nichols Prize jury chose the first Muslim leader to receive the ULI J.C. Nichols Prize for Visionaries in Urban Development. Aside from the geographical focus of his work, His Highness the Aga Khan was considered an unconventional choice for several reasons. He is not a developer, builder, or architect, nor does he have a formal relationship with the Urban Land Institute.

Rather, the Aga Khan is the 49th spiritual leader of the Ismaili Muslims, a branch of Shi'a Islam and a faith community of 20 million people spanning 25 nations. He is also a direct descendant of the Prophet Muhammad through his ancestors, among them, the Fatimids, who built the city of Cairo.

As a spiritual leader and humanitarian, the Aga Khan sees his primary goal as improving the physical environment and quality of life for not only his followers but also for all people in the developing world—with a particular emphasis on impoverished communities in Asia and Africa.

The Aga Khan interprets his work as a combination of *din* and *dunya*, the melding of spiritual and material aspects of life. Quoting a verse from the Qur'an, the Aga Khan framed his philosophy in a 2008 interview: "You should leave the world in a better environment than you found it. You have a responsibility to the legacy of God's creation of the world, to improve that legacy from generation to generation."

Born in Geneva in 1936, the Aga Khan spent his early childhood in Nairobi, Kenya, attended boarding school in Switzerland, and graduated from Harvard University with a BA honors degree in Islamic history. He makes his home in Picardie, France.

Since assuming the Imamat (office of the Imam) in 1957 at age 20, the Aga Khan has pursued his mandate through the Aga Khan Development Network (AKDN), a group of agencies with an annual budget of approximately $600 million devoted to a stunning array of secular development work: historic and cultural preservation, humanitarian response, microfinancing, housing, and environmental initiatives. The AKDN has also established schools, universities, and hospitals in societies where Muslims have either a

Opposite: His Highness the Aga Khan visits the Humayun Tomb and Sunder Nursery Complex in New Delhi, India. *(Ram Rahman)*

"Nothing serious, long-lived, or self-sustaining can be achieved unless the suitability of the land that is involved and the economic conditions under which it becomes available are consistent both with long-range social purposes and sensible financial objectives."

HIS HIGHNESS THE AGA KHAN · 2011 NICHOLS LAUREATE

majority or minority presence and all people are seeking better opportunities and healthy, happy lives.

Societies of developing nations often appear in the news because of political crises and civil war, yet the Aga Khan seeks to promote a different image, one that values pluralism, tolerance, and peace. He does so through the creation of universities, academies, health centers, and hospitals as well as through institutions such as the Aga Khan Museum and Global Centre for Pluralism. He also pursues those values through the creation of public open spaces and the large-scale renovations of historic sites that allow communities to gather and individuals to have quiet moments of reflection. From Afghanistan to Mali, from Cairo to Delhi, the Aga Khan encourages ordinary citizens to take pride in their cultural heritage and to feel inspired to create change in their own lives.

Therefore, it is through the work of the AKDN that the Aga Khan epitomizes the mission of ULI to create and sustain thriving communities worldwide and truly reflects what the Nichols Prize seeks to recognize: visionaries who seek to improve the world around them.

"Through the Aga Khan Development Network, progress and improvements to communities have been undertaken in over 30 countries," said James DeFrancia, a member of the Nichols Prize jury and principal of Lowe Enterprises in Aspen, Colorado. "The efforts of the Aga Khan have globally contributed to a quality built environment, strengthening both communities and society at large."

To Nichols juror Bart Harvey III, the selection of the Aga Khan signaled an evolution of ULI itself—"the start of ULI reaching out" to developing nations, he said, where rapid urbanization and population growth signify a shift in political and economic influence away from the West.

"What he represents is the developing world and very poor communities that are really going to determine the fate of the world," Harvey said. How the built environment will work for them is a question the Aga Khan passionately pursues.

• • •

The Nichols jury singled out two AKDN agencies in its selection of the Aga Khan: the Aga Khan Planning and Building Services (AKPBS) and the Aga Khan Trust for Culture (AKTC).

First established in Pakistan in 1980, the AKPBS has developed numerous initiatives to improve the living conditions of people in underserved regions. As the Aga Khan described the agency's goal: "A proper home can bridge that terrible gap between poverty and a better future."

AKPBS's work in Northern Pakistan is noteworthy for its enormous impact on the lives of poor families in the Hunza Valley's remote mountain villages. Because of a lack of gas supplies, villagers use wood as their main source of cooking and heating fuel, causing massive deforestation, soil erosion, and flooding. Villagers experience respiratory problems as a result of excessive smoke from wood fires used in their poorly ventilated homes.

AKPBS developed low-cost and energy-efficient technologies to remedy this situation. The agency introduced metal stoves with chimneys and roof-hatch windows that carry smoke out of the house, improving ventilation in village houses. In addition, the metal stoves include a pipe that connects water barrels so villagers can access hot water on demand. The agency also developed floor and wall insulation for better temperature control inside homes. Villagers receive a subsidy if they purchase all four technologies in a package.

The technologies spurred the local economy. AKPBS contracted with local craftsmen to manufacture the stoves, window hatches, and insulation material, providing them with a steady source of income and new job skills. The agency hired local women as resource workers to go from home to home, educating peers on the health and environmental benefits of the technologies.

"People really like the fact that they can heat and cook at the same time—they don't need to use two lots of wood," reported Bibi Safina, an AKPBS resource worker who earned a salary for her outreach efforts.

Northern Pakistan is also prone to massive earthquakes; in response, AKPBS developed public education campaigns on seismic safety and disaster preparedness among villagers and introduced new building techniques and materials to retrofit homes. Finally, AKPBS in Pakistan has lowered mortality rates in the area formerly known as the North-West Frontier Province through its water sanitation programs. By installing water supply infrastructure, creating health and hygiene education programs, and increasing potable water supplies, the agency reduced the number of waterborne diseases and improved water quality.

• • •

"The efforts of the Aga Khan have globally contributed to a quality built environment, strengthening both communities and society at large."

JAMES M. DEFRANCIA • 2011 JURY MEMBER

The jury also identified the Aga Khan Trust for Culture, including the Aga Khan Award for Architecture, as exemplifying the spirit of the Nichols Prize.

Through its Historic Cities Programme, the AKTC undertakes large-scale conservation projects of historic sites to further multiple goals: renovate architectural treasures to boost both tourism and community engagement; provide a springboard to local economic development activity and public health and educational programs; and establish cultural initiatives that puts the long-term sustainability of the site in the hands of the community. In a 2013 speech inaugurating the Hazrat Nizamuddin Basti urban renewal project in Delhi, India, the Aga Khan explained that historic preservation could stimulate local economics and foster a sense of pride and ownership of cultural heritage.

"Rather than being a drain on fragile economies, as some once feared, investment in cultural legacies can be a powerful agent in improving the quality of human life," he said. "The impact of such projects can begin by diversifying local economies, expanding employment, and teaching new skills."

From its start in 2007, the Nizamuddin project exemplified what the Aga Khan called a "multi-input approach" to community development. By combining historic conservation with environmental stewardship of local landscapes, vocational skills training in local craft making, and the expansion of schools and health clinics in the surrounding *basti,* or adjacent neighborhood, the project sought to rebuild both physical structures and human lives. The AKTC partnered with the Archaeological Survey of India, the Ford Foundation, and the Delhi government to complete the project in 2013.

Covering a roughly 200-acre area in the heart of Delhi, the site is home to a large concentration of Mughal-era monuments, including Humayun's Tomb, a UNESCO World Heritage Site. Master stone and tile craftsmen restored the tomb and its gardens to their former glory and at the same time trained local youth in traditional techniques. Thousands of new tree and plant species were planted in the nearby Sunder Nursery, creating a microhabitat for native birds and insects and a truly open space for residents. In the basti, an early childhood education center and a maternal health clinic opened, offering better services and job training to residents. Two new community toilets were built as well.

Through its multifaceted approach, the Historic Cities Programme "brings together the technical skills of architectural conservators, urban planners, and development specialists and promotes microfinance initiatives, vocational training, and health care," said Luis Monreal, the AKTC's general manager.

Nearly 20 years earlier, AKTC undertook a similar urban renewal project in Cairo, a city established by descendants of Fatima, the Prophet Muhammad's daughter. In 1999, AKTC broke ground on a public park in a part of the city that had been a garbage dump for 500 years. The result, Al-Azhar Park is a 74-acre landscaped gem that gives Cairo residents a respite from the city's hectic pace and politically charged atmosphere. Monument conservation, microcredit programs, housing rehabilitation, and infrastructural improvements benefited the adjacent neighborhood, Darb Al-Ahmar, where poverty, illiteracy, and drug dealing had held the community back.

Opposite:

Top: His Highness the Aga Khan and President Yoweri Museveni of Uganda plant a tree at the inauguration of the Bujagali power plant in 2012. *(Gary Otte)*

Bottom right: Aga Khan Planning & Building Services funded the construction of fuel-efficient stoves with warming facilities attached in rural communities in India and Pakistan. Not only are these stoves energy efficient, but they are also smoke-free, which reduces the incidence of respiratory illnesses in women and children significantly. *(Aga Khan Development Network)*

Bottom left: An aerial view of the Al-Azhar Park project in Cairo. *(Kareem Ibrahim)*

Top: The Aga Khan Award for Architecture recognizes achievement in global architecture across the Muslim world. A recipient of the award in 2004, the Petronas Tower is the centerpiece of a mixed-use complex in the heart of Kuala Lumpur, Malaysia. Designed by Cesar Pelli and Associates, the towers are among the tallest buildings in the world. Their elegant form dominates the Malaysian skyline and affirms the country's position on the world stage. *(Aga Khan Trust for Culture)*

Bottom: The Kahere Poultry Farming School, which won the Aga Khan Award for Architecture in 2001, is located in Koliagbe, Guinea, and was designed by Finnish architecture firm Heikkinen-Komonen Architects. *(Aga Khan Trust for Culture)*

"Lots of people said this would not work, that Egypt is not ready for this yet—a public park in its true sense," said Mohammed el-Mikawi, former general manager of Aga Khan Cultural Services in Egypt, in a podcast. Yet the park's popularity has proven the opposite, he added. "We have visitors of all ages, social backgrounds. It's just a magnificent public space."

• • •

His Highness the Aga Khan's interest in Islamic architecture isn't limited to historic sites—it extends to contemporary expressions across vastly different contexts and cultures. Beginning in 1977 and occurring every three years, the Aga Khan Award for Architecture, an AKTC program, recognizes examples of architectural excellence across the Muslim world.

There seem to be no boundaries in the types of structures it recognizes—awardees include the landscape architects, masons, and planners behind the ultramodern Petronas Towers in Kuala Lumpur (2004), the Kahere Eila Poultry Farming School in Koliagbe, Guinea (2001), and an Islamic cemetery for the Muslim community in Altach, Austria (2013). Alongside César Pelli for his Petronas Towers design, Iranian architect Nader Khalili also received the award in 2004 for prototypes of emergency housing made from sandbags held together by barbed wire in dome-like structures for seismic protection.

The choice generated controversy among jurors, some of whom viewed the sandbag shelters as impractical. The jury ultimately supported the project, commending it for "using extremely inexpensive means to provide safe homes that can be built quickly," according to the jury's citation referenced in *Under the Eaves of Architecture: The Aga Khan: Builder and Patron* by art historian Philip Jodidio.

The Aga Khan's motivation in creating the award was in part brought about by his desire to encourage architectural ingenuity in the Muslim world that neither mimicked Western forms nor was purely a rehash of Islamic architecture's golden age. According to an interview with Jodidio, the Aga Khan was determined to use the award to expand the definition of quality beyond what he called "architectured" buildings—those that were undertaken in terms understood by Western and Western-trained architects only.

"The vast majority of buildings in the developing world are not 'architectured' buildings in the sense of the Western profession," he said. "That does mean that quality buildings do not happen. They happen through a whole series of different processes. . . . There is a whole body of inherited knowledge in developing countries, and in the Islamic world in particular, which is not driven by Western standards of architecture. . . . Very early on there was a consensus that the Aga Khan Award could not be just for 'architectured' buildings, it had to be an award for quality buildings no matter what the process of their creation."

Sharing Lessons of the Aga Khan Development Network

This is an excerpt from the speech by His Highness the Aga Khan at the ULI Europe Annual Conference Leadership Dinner, held in Paris on January 31, 2012.

It is a distinct pleasure for me to be here this evening—and I would like to begin by expressing my renewed and deep thanks to the Urban Land Institute for presenting to me the J.C. Nichols Prize at your 75th anniversary conference last fall.

As you may know, my interest in urban planning has something of an historical precedent—going back 1,000 years—to the founding of the city of Cairo by my ancestors, the Fatimid Imam-Caliphs.

The Fatimids are remembered for drawing, pluralistically, on the widest array of talent, from all cultures, in developing a great civilization. One of the ways I have tried to reflect this history has been to encourage the development of world-class planning and design resources, including programs such as the Aga Khan Award for Architecture and the Aga Khan Program for Islamic Architecture at Harvard University and the Massachusetts Institute of Technology.

For my comments this evening, it was suggested that I share some of the lessons the Aga Khan Development Network has learned from its 50 and more years of work, essentially in the developing countries of East and West Africa, South and Central Asia, and the Middle East. And it seemed that one of the subjects that I might discuss with you this evening, and which bridges our interests of today and perhaps our destinies for tomorrow, is the subject of "impact investing."

As you know, a wide spectrum of investors has been increasingly involved in impact investing, using a diverse array of assets, employing highly disciplined due diligence and accounting analyses, and pursuing a balanced mix of financial, social, economic, and environmental goals.

It has been exciting to see the volume of such investments growing substantially in recent years—with growth expected to reach around 500 billion U.S. dollars in the next ten years.

So let me briefly make three observations.

His Highness the Aga Khan accepted the ULI J.C. Nichols Prize at the ULI Europe Annual Conference in Paris in 2012. *(Karla Gowlett)*

Number one—to the best of our knowledge, there has been relatively little history as yet of impact investing in the property development field. To me, this could mean a great deal of untapped, upside potential. What now is needed most are knowledgeable intermediaries who fully comprehend the realities of business risk and reward in the property field—while also understanding what it takes to improve the quality of life for the engaged populations. I believe that both the Urban Land Institute and the Aga Khan Development Network can bring a great deal to this stimulating discussion.

My second point is that the power of impact investing is only beginning to be seen in the less developed parts of the world. We have witnessed in recent decades the rapid, exciting development of newly industrialized countries—especially along the Pacific Rim, and we have heralded the potentials of the so-called BRIC

[Brazil, Russia, India, and China] countries. But my suggestion to you tonight is that there are many places in the less developed world that now hold similar promise.

Our network has been working in these places for over half a century. Many of them have experienced the heavy legacies of colonialism, the rigidities of Marxism, the misleading hopes of various new nationalisms, and the naive promises of undisciplined and sometimes greedy capitalism. Meanwhile, inexperienced democracies have also struggled to find workable forms of coalition government, a global issue today.

These fragilities still exist, but to a much lesser extent. Over time, our faith has been reinforced in the potential of these regions, especially for competent impact investing. Indeed, I would say that sustainable development that improves the quality of life for the peoples of the developing world will depend in the end on efforts that make sense both socially and financially.

As this process goes forward, the disciplines and resources of the property investment community will be particularly well suited to such opportunities.

This is true, first, because of the growing demand for property in the developing world, reflecting not only higher birth rates but also the rapid pace of urbanization. We remember that dramatic economic development in the industrialized world was invariably accompanied by accelerated urbanization. Today, in less developed countries, population growth and urbanization are combining with the rapid growth of the middle class as well as with climatic and geographic constraints on the supply of land—and the likely result is a continuing increase in property values.

This scenario will be played out not only in the great capital cities of the developing world, but also, most probably, in its "secondary" cities.

There is another critically important factor that I would emphasize this evening—and that is the increasing importance for these populations of civil society institutions. By civil society, I mean those nongovernmental institutions which serve great public purposes. They include organizations devoted to education, to culture, to health, and to environmental improvement; they embrace commercial, labor, professional, and ethnic associations, as well as religion and media. Improving the scale and the competence of civil society is a focal goal for the entirety of the Aga Khan Development Network.

Even when governments are fragile or disappointing, strong civil society organizations generally remain as key drivers of development. Strengthening the pillars of civil society is the most effective way I know of ensuring a positive social impact in the developing world.

Let me spotlight one other helpful variable in this equation—and that is the expanding opportunity for regional investment—across national frontiers. Strategies that cross arbitrary political boundaries to engage cross-border communities of cooperation can enhance growth opportunities—while also spreading risks more widely.

My third and final message is simply to explain why the Aga Khan Development Network can be a valuable resource in discussing these investment opportunities.

Let me sketch out quickly the work that we do. AKDN is active in over 30 developing countries. We employ some 80,000 people, supported by tens of thousands of volunteers. And one of the characteristics of development in the third world is voluntary service. These volunteers and others work in a vast array of fields, reflecting what we call a multi-input approach. The majority of projects are in the not-for-profit sector, ranging from the building of bridges and the restoration of cultural heritage sites to far-flung institutions in the fields of health and education. The Aga Khan University, for example, has the leading health sciences faculty in Pakistan and now has 13 campuses in eight countries, including major teaching hospitals which are shaping the future of health care in Pakistan and in Kenya. They use surpluses generated by one set of services to subsidize care for poorer patients as well as scholarships for medical and nursing students. Meanwhile, our health services programs include medical outreach centers in many hundreds, literally hundreds, of rural and urban communities.

And in Tajikistan, the Kyrgyz Republic, and Kazakhstan, the University of Central Asia has served some 30,000 students since its foundation in 2006.

At the same time, a broad portfolio of projects moves forward under the aegis of the Aga Khan Trust for Culture, involving fields such as architecture, music, parks, and the restoration of historic sites.

Another large portion of our work is entrepreneurial, channeled through the Aga Khan Fund for Economic Development. These ventures, over 90 of them, are held to rigorous profit and loss disciplines. All surpluses they generate are reinvested in business expansion or in efforts to aid the less fortunate. These ventures range from banking and insurance companies to the tourism and leisure sector, from food processing and clothing manufacture to telecommunications and media, from energy generation to aviation—and, more recently, a microlending program which now has some 300 branches in 13 countries.

Let me illustrate one or two specific examples. I will start with our lead investment in a hydropower project which will almost double the supply of electric power to the grid in Uganda. In Afghanistan, a mobile phone company called Roshan is transforming the likely shape of the country's postconflict situation by offering not only reliable communications to connect the whole country, but also sophisticated tele-medicine and financial services—and that is happening today in Afghanistan.

The Serena Hotel group—with facilities now in eight countries in Africa and Central Asia staffed almost entirely by local employees—contributes significantly to the diversification of their national economies. And let me mention Nation Media Group launched over 50 years ago, and it is now a publicly traded entity and one of the largest independent multimedia companies in Africa. And there are many other exciting examples.

I mention this wide spectrum of social, cultural, and economic initiatives to reinforce what I have said earlier about the potential for sensible impact investing in places which have not been in the investment spotlight.

We envision the launch of additional major projects in the coming decade—including efforts to strengthen the education and health systems of the less developed world—opening new capital initiatives and expanding existing ones, while also providing opportunities for operating partnerships. As we move forward, we are encouraged by the growing interest of other potential partners, including international government agencies which often provide concessionary financing.

As you can see, the Aga Khan Development Network attaches central importance to the role, in the world in which we work, of property impact investment.

Whether one is developing a university, a hospital, a school, a park, an historical site, a commercial enterprise, a municipal facility, or a regional network of institutions—land planning, building development, and financing are fundamental variables.

Nothing serious, long-lived, or self-sustaining can be achieved unless the suitability of the land that is involved and the economic conditions under which it becomes available are consistent both with long-range social purposes and sensible financial objectives.

Property impact investing represents an exciting new funding niche, positioned halfway between enterprise financing and development funding. It is my hope that as all of us come to share, more and more, our knowledge and experience, we might also share in some new, highly original, and satisfactory outcomes. ∎

2012

PETER WALKER

Forging the Renaissance of Landscape Architecture

Originally published in October 2012

(PWP Landscape Architecture)

Opposite: The National September 11 Memorial. *(PWP Landscape Architecture)*

The sound of waterfalls frames the footprints where the Twin Towers once stood. Visitors reflect on the impact of the events that shook the world as they contemplate the names of every person who died in the 2001 and 1993 attacks inscribed into bronze panels edging the memorial's pools. This powerful reminder of the largest loss of life resulting from a foreign attack on American soil is punctuated by the soothing array of swamp white oaks among which the survivor tree from the September 11 attack grows again. This contemplative space—separate from the usual sights and sounds of a bustling metropolis, and yet deeply engrained in its urban fabric—illustrates the imprint of Peter Walker's work in the built environment.

Walker's practice as a world-renowned landscape architect, founder of PWP Landscape Architecture in Berkeley, California, has earned him the Urban Land Institute's highest honor, the ULI J.C. Nichols Prize for Visionaries in Urban Development, making him the first landscape architect to receive it in the award's 13-year history. The $100,000 annual prize, which honors ULI founder and legendary Kansas City, Missouri, developer J.C. Nichols, recognizes an individual whose career demonstrates a longtime commitment to the highest standards of responsible development.

Walker, whose career spans more than five decades, is widely recognized as one of the most accomplished and influential landscape architects of his time, forging the renaissance of landscape architecture as a discipline. The scope of his work is expansive, ranging from the design of small gardens to the planning of cities around the globe, with a particular emphasis on corporate headquarters, plazas, cultural gardens, academic campuses, and urban regeneration projects. Exploring the relationships among art, culture, and context, Walker challenges traditional concepts of landscape design. His work reflects his lifelong dedication to creating open space that will be shared and cherished for generations.

"A public space should be flexible enough so that people can use it for all sorts of reasons. The goal is to bring enough importance to the space to create a great memory for all who visit."

PETER WALKER • 2012 NICHOLS LAUREATE

Left: Proposed redevelopment of Constitution Gardens on the National Mall in Washington, D.C. *(PWP Landscape Architecture)*

Right: More than 50 years ago, Peter Walker, in partnership with Hideo Sasaki, created the setting for a statue that remains a focal point of children's activity in Central Park. The sculpted group of Alice, the Mad Hatter, the White Rabbit, and the Dormouse is surrounded by a ring of benches that have drawn Manhattan families for generations. *(PWP Landscape Architecture)*

The jury for the 2012 Nichols Prize chose Walker as the 2012 laureate recognizing the importance of lively, appealing public spaces as an essential component of thriving communities worldwide. "For ULI, choosing Peter Walker makes a statement about the importance of landscape architecture to the built environment and especially the necessity of providing sustainable systems, both built and natural," says John Bucksbaum, founder of Bucksbaum Retail Properties in Chicago and Nichols Prize jury chair.

Walker cofounded Sasaki, Walker, and Associates in 1957 and opened its West Coast office. Renamed the SWA Group in 1976, the firm became a multidisciplinary office with an international reputation for excellence in environmental design, with Walker as principal and chairman of the board. In 1983, he formed Peter Walker and Partners, now known as PWP Landscape Architecture.

"As a professional, he designed many innovative places for people; as a teacher, he trained many landscape architects in understanding and creating responsible developments; and as a friend and mentor, he raised all our sights for what the built environment could be in harmony with the natural world," says Kalvin Platt, consulting principal and board member of the SWA Group, reflecting on more than 20 years of work alongside Walker.

Walker's thoughtful approach to place making has been highly praised as reflecting both the collaborative aspiration of his practice and the public impact of his work. Prominent projects include the National September 11 Memorial, Reflecting Absence, in New York City; the Nasher Foundation Sculpture Garden in Dallas; Sony Center in Berlin; Millennium Park in Sydney; and most recently he has been selected to lead the redevelopment of Constitution Gardens on the National Mall in Washington, D.C.

Walker's approach has been described as minimalist—one that encourages ample creativity in how a space is used. "A public space should be flexible enough so that people can use it for all sorts of reasons. The goal is to bring enough importance to the space to create a great memory for all who visit," he says. "I wanted to create spaces that are more 'universal.' If you make spaces more general, more generous, then people can decide what they want to do with them and change them over time."

Through his writings, teachings, and work, Walker has advanced the level of professionalism in landscape architecture and has influenced generations of landscape architects and people in related professions. He played an essential role in the Graduate School of Design at Harvard University as both the chairman of the Landscape Architecture

SINCE RECEIVING THE NICHOLS PRIZE IN 2012

Peter Walker has continued to exert a significant influence in the field of landscape architecture and how it contributes to create thriving communities.

In addition to his academic commitment, he has continued leading the work of PWP Landscape Architecture with projects around the globe, such as the the site development of Ciudad de Victoria in the Philippines and the ambitious Barangaroo project in Sydney, Australia, which will dramatically transform the city's access to the harbor and enable further economic development.

During his keynote presentation at the 2014 ULI Transformational Urban Open Space forum, Walker emphasized the commitment that Barangaroo represents to generate an open and communal sense of place. The project's 14.8 acres include the re-creation of 1836 Millers Point Headland—a mixed-use area with a cultural and civic park as well as commercial office and residential towers—and a waterfront promenade connecting pedestrians to the entire harbor edge from the Rocks through Barangaroo to Darling Harbor. The design carefully looks at the area's Aboriginal history and its connection to nearby Goat Island and surrounding headlands. The planned public domain accommodates a wide variety of public activities and opportunities, from intimate nature walks to active recreation, picnics, and a schedule of festivals, concerts, and New Year's Eve events. All the potential uses are connected by the Foreshore Promenade, which also engages waterside activity. ■

The Barangaroo project in Sydney re-creates a historic headland on an abandoned dock in Sydney Harbor, incorporating an underground cultural center and a public garage. Extracted on the site, large blocks of sandstone—a material that references both the topography and the building material of early Sydney—are starting to mark the edges of the harbor with tidal pools. (PWP Landscape Architecture)

Department and the acting director of the Urban Design Program. He was also head of the Department of Landscape Architecture at the University of California at Berkeley from 1997 to 1999.

"Pete's generosity in design is notable," says Thomas Oslund, principal of oslund.and.assoc. "He has enabled me and many others to move our profession far beyond conventional thought through his dedication to design education, his execution of design ideas, and the openness to share his design discoveries with all of us."

"Choosing Peter Walker makes a statement about the importance of landscape architecture to the built environment and especially the necessity of providing sustainable systems, both built and natural."

JOHN BUCKSBAUM • 2012 JURY CHAIR

Walker has also served as a pivotal consultant and adviser to numerous public agencies and institutions, including the Sydney 2000 Olympic Coordination Authority, the Redevelopment Agency of San Francisco, the Port Authority of San Diego, Stanford University, the University of California, the University of Washington, and the American Academy in Rome.

Through his career, Peter Walker has transformed the thinking about human environments. His legacy of elegant and understated open space and his influence on practitioners worldwide reflect an unwavering commitment to the standards of excellence that J.C. Nichols represented and make him a deserving recipient of the 2012 ULI J.C. Nichols Prize for Visionaries in Urban Development.

Opposite:

Top: Jamison Square, Portland, Oregon. *(PWP Landscape Architecture)*

Bottom: Nasher Sculpture Center Garden in Dallas, Texas. *(PWP Landscape Architecture)*

2013

J. RONALD TERWILLIGER

Offering Hope through Housing

Originally published in October 2013

Opposite: The outdoor play area at Via Verde, a mixed-use, mixed-income community in the Bronx, New York. Developed by the Jonathan Rose Companies and Phipps Houses, the project was among the 2012 winners of the ULI Terwilliger Center's Jack Kemp Workforce Housing Models of Excellence Awards. It is the type of housing championed by ULI J.C. Nichols Prize laureate J. Ronald Terwilliger. *(David Sunberg)*

J. Ronald Terwilliger has fond memories of growing up in a working-class neighborhood in Arlington, Virginia, in the 1940s and 1950s. He played outside with the other kids on his street until well after dark. He walked or biked wherever he needed to go. He did not feel rich or poor; he felt he was part of the community. That sense of belonging, seeded in the comfort of being able to equate housing with home and security, would ultimately shape a commitment he made decades later to expand and improve housing options in communities around the world.

Now an internationally renowned housing expert and a champion of affordable and workforce housing, Terwilliger, 72, a former ULI chairman and the chairman emeritus of Trammell Crow Residential, has been selected as the 2013 recipient of the Urban Land Institute J.C. Nichols Prize for Visionaries in Urban Development. The Institute's highest honor, the Nichols Prize recognizes a person, or a person representing an institution, who has demonstrated a longtime commitment to the creation of communities that prosper by providing a high quality of life for all residents, and that reflect the highest standards of design and development. The $100,000 prize honors the legacy of Kansas City, Missouri, developer J.C. Nichols, a founding ULI member considered one of America's most creative entrepreneurs in land use during the first half of the 1900s.

Terwilliger, founder of the ULI Terwilliger Center for Housing, is being recognized for his extraordinary civic and philanthropic efforts to raise awareness of decent housing as a basic human need, with a particular emphasis on increasing the supply of housing that is both affordable to the workforce and close to transit and employment centers. "In my professional life, I've seen housing strengthen health, education, families, communities, and economies," Terwilliger says. "In my philanthropic life, I've tried to demonstrate my belief that hope begins with access to a decent, affordable home. I want to help ensure a leveraged, sustained impact beyond my lifetime and inspire others to make the commitment to support affordable housing."

"What separates Ron from a great many people is that not only does he contribute financial resources to what he's involved in and what he feels is important, but the fact

"*In my philanthropic life, I've tried to demonstrate my belief that hope begins with access to a decent, affordable home. I want to help ensure a leveraged, sustained impact beyond my lifetime and inspire others to make the commitment to support affordable housing.*"

J. RONALD TERWILLIGER • 2013 NICHOLS LAUREATE

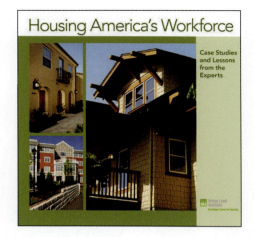

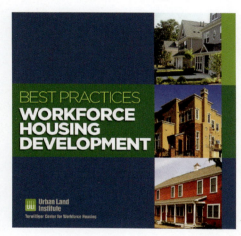

Since the creation of the ULI Terwilliger Center for Housing, ULI has released several publications related to affordable and workforce housing, including the award-winning *Housing America's Workforce*, which showcases best practices in mixed-income housing development.

that he is willing to give his time, his knowledge, and his experience," says Nichols Prize jury chairman John L. Bucksbaum, chief executive officer of Bucksbaum Retail Properties LLC in Chicago. "Very few people do this. It's a testament to the type of person Ron is."

"The Nichols Prize is about community building, insight, and visionary development. It's a highly visible symbol of ULI. Ron Terwilliger touches all those bases," adds jury member Ronald A. Altoon, founder and partner at Altoon Partners LLP in Los Angeles.

Terwilliger's advocacy work in the arena of housing affordability has built momentum over the past two decades, evolving into a full-time commitment in the latter 2000s as he wound down his highly successful career as Trammell Crow Residential's chief executive officer. As ULI chairman from 1999 to 2001, he regularly spoke and wrote about the need for affordable and mixed-income housing, and at the conclusion of his term, he provided ULI with an endowment to support a senior resident fellow position focused on housing. In 2007, Terwilliger committed $5 million—the largest individual gift ever contributed to ULI at the time—to establish the ULI J. Ronald Terwilliger Center for Housing, which engages in a multifaceted program of work to further the development of mixed-income, mixed-use communities with a full spectrum of housing. Also in 2007, he contributed $5 million to Enterprise Community Partners, where he currently serves as chairman of the board, to support affordable housing development through the Enterprise Terwilliger Fund.

"Ron shows up. He's caring; he's concerned. He has a way of cutting through the rhetoric and getting to a solution," says jury member James D. Klingbeil, former chairman of ULI and the ULI Foundation, and chairman and chief executive officer of Klingbeil Capital Management in San Francisco. "He's really moved the whole quest for affordable housing forward with his money, his time, his intuition, and his leadership. Ron basically embodies the process of sharing and giving back, which is what ULI is all about."

Terwilliger's interest in affordable housing became a global pursuit as a result of his increased involvement with Habitat for Humanity International in the 2000s. In 2009, he announced a $100 million legacy gift to the housing organization—the largest donation Habitat has ever received from an individual—which will help an estimated 60,000 low-income families around the world improve their housing. A member of Habitat's board of directors since 2000, he has served as the board chairman for the organization and is the global chair for its "A World of Hope: It Starts at Home" fundraising campaign.

"Ron cares deeply about housing issues in the United States, but he has grown a huge heart for how desperate the situation is in other countries around the world," says Habitat chief executive officer Jonathan Reckford. (Habitat estimates that more than one billion people worldwide lack access to adequate housing.) "He understands that housing is as important as education and medical care [as a fundamental need]. . . . They are all inextricably linked together. It is quite rare for someone to be so passionate about affordable housing. Ron's commitment to impacting the affordable housing environment both domestically and internationally is extraordinary."

Terwilliger was named the National Housing Council's Housing Person of the Year in 2009 in recognition of his inspirational leadership. "Ron gets the value of a house being a home—a home you can be proud of," explains Nichols jury member F. Barton Harvey, board member of Fannie Mae in Washington, D.C. "He has put his success and his reputation on the line to really work for the inclusion of those that have the least in our society."

Terwilliger's interest in affordable housing (generally targeted to households making 50 percent or less of area median income) and in workforce housing (generally targeted to those making up to 120 percent of area median income) is rooted in a combination of experiences—his modest upbringing in northern Virginia; his work in the early 1970s as a young professional for Charles Fraser at Sea Pines Resort on Hilton Head Island, South Carolina; and 23 years (from 1986 through 2009) as the chief executive of Trammell Crow Residential, which under his leadership became the nation's largest developer of multifamily housing. (While at Trammell Crow Residential, based in Atlanta at the time, Terwilliger chaired the Atlanta Neighborhood Development Partnership, working closely with then-Atlanta Mayor Shirley Franklin.) Each of these experiences, in different ways, reinforced his decision to champion mixed-income housing as a way to increase the availability of attractive affordable and workforce housing.

At Sea Pines, Fraser's team learned to think of housing development not just in terms of building places to live, but also as a way to provide a total living experience for people in a broad income range. "At Sea Pines, Charles [Fraser] taught us to think in terms of what it was like to live in a place, and I believe this helped shape Ron's commitment to not just provide shelter, but to provide a total residential experience," explains former

SINCE RECEIVING THE NICHOLS PRIZE IN 2013

J. Ronald Terwilliger has continued to raise awareness of decent housing as a basic human need, with a particular emphasis on increasing the supply of high-quality affordable rental and workforce housing.

In 2013, Terwilliger presented the 14th annual John T. Dunlop Lecture at the Harvard Graduate School of Design. Terwilliger's speech, titled "Housing America's Increasingly Diverse Population," emphasized the nation's changing demographics and provided recommendations for changes in housing policy. "Our nation is undergoing a profound demographic transformation," said Terwilliger. "These demographic trends will alter the types of homes Americans will choose. They will have enormous implications for housing affordability. And I believe they will require fundamental changes in housing policy to match the new realities in the marketplace."

In 2014, Terwilliger was elected a member of the Horatio Alger Association in recognition of his commitment to philanthropy and higher education while overcoming significant personal challenges to achieve his success. Also in 2014, Terwilliger made a leadership gift of $15 million to the U.S. Naval Academy. This gift was given to construct a building celebrating student athletes at the Naval Academy, a college that emphasizes moral, mental, and physical excellence. Terwilliger also agreed to cochair the Naval Academy's $400 million capital campaign.

Along with serving as chair for the ULI Terwilliger Center for Housing, Terwilliger continues to serve as chair of Enterprise Community Partners as well as global campaign chairman for Habitat for Humanity International. Terwilliger's newest contribution to national housing policy, the J. Ronald Terwilliger Foundation for Housing America's Families, was to be unveiled in fall 2014. ■

ULI Chairman James J. Chaffin Jr., who worked with Terwilliger at Sea Pines and is now chairman of Chaffin Light Management LLC in Okatie, South Carolina. In the decades since, Terwilliger's focus has been on how to "provide places for families to live affordably and enjoy a high quality of life," Chaffin adds.

Under Terwilliger's leadership at Trammell Crow Residential, the company built more than 250,000 multifamily rental units. And while it did use incentives from a 1981 tax law to build some below-market-rate units, the majority of the company's product was—and continues to be—market rate.

"At Trammell Crow, we were serving a clientele who could afford market-rate housing. But to a large extent we were not reaching a lot of people [priced out of the apartments]," Terwilliger says. His years in development convinced him of the potential for the private sector to produce attractive low-cost housing—if provided with incentives to mitigate problems such as rising land costs, zoning limitations, and other risk factors. "When properly motivated, the private sector is very efficient and certainly the best equipped to create this type of housing," he explains.

For several years, Terwilliger has advocated incentives at various levels of government to encourage affordable and workforce housing development, such as the adoption of inclusionary zoning requirements by local jurisdictions and the expansion of the Low-Income Housing Tax Credit (enacted in 1987), which is the main federal incentive still available to spur private development of affordable housing. "We as a country need to allocate more resources to provide decent housing for every American family—not for the purpose of eliminating personal responsibility, but to offer people who need help a hand up," he says.

Two years ago, Terwilliger was asked to serve on the Bipartisan Policy Center's Housing Commission, created following the housing industry collapse to help reform the nation's housing policy and address near- and long-term challenges facing the housing sector. Earlier this year, the commission issued recommendations to the Obama administration and the U.S. Congress on scaling back the government's role in the nation's housing finance system and revising housing assistance programs to better meet the needs of America's most vulnerable households.

"Ron is a voice for fairness, a voice for balance in American housing policy, and a voice for facing up to our most pressing housing needs in realistic ways," says Henry Cisneros, former secretary of the U.S. Department of Housing and Urban Development and a cochair of the Housing Commission. When the commission was preparing its policy recommendations, Terwilliger was the most ardent supporter for a better balance between federal subsidies that support homeownership and those that support rental housing— specifically affordable rentals, Cisneros says. "No one on the commission was more insistent or persuasive than Ron. His arguments were unassailable. Ron has a big heart and a sense of fairness, and that, matched with his experience and power of analysis, is a powerful combination to get things done."

Nichols Prize jury member and former ULI Chairman Marilyn J. Taylor also serves on the Housing Commission. "Ron is one of the most effective and influential advocates of

Opposite:

Top: Terwilliger works on a Habitat for Humanity home. *(Habitat for Humanity International)*

Bottom left: Terwilliger with former U.S. President Jimmy Carter, who has been involved with the Habitat organization for nearly 30 years. *(Habitat for Humanity International)*

Bottom right: Terwilliger announcing creation of the ULI Terwilliger Center for Housing in 2007. "If we do not act now to bring housing and jobs closer together, we will seriously impede the ability of America's cities to compete with cities around the world," he said.

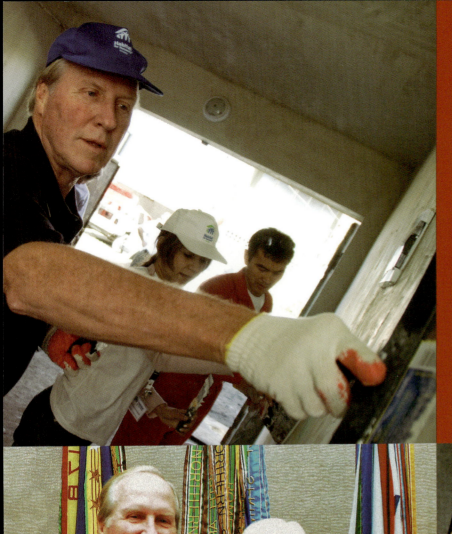

"Ron shows up. He's caring, he's concerned. He has a way of cutting through the rhetoric and getting to a solution."

JAMES D. KLINGBEIL • 2013 JURY MEMBER

Rhode Island Row, a 274-unit mixed-use, mixed-income community adjacent to the Rhode Island Avenue Metrorail station in Washington, D.C. It was among the 2012 winners of the ULI Terwilliger Center's Jack Kemp Workforce Housing Models of Excellence Awards. *(Brian Rennie, Bozzuto Construction)*

forward-looking housing policies I've ever known," says Taylor, dean of and Paley Professor at the University of Pennsylvania School of Design in Philadelphia. "He is showing public leaders how private [sector] investment in housing can achieve the longstanding elusive goal of decent housing and a suitable living environment for every American."

"I know how important it is to give people a chance," Terwilliger says. "And that chance starts with a decent house a family can afford in a suitable neighborhood. . . . If the first half of your business life is for success, the second half should be for significance. I'm in my second half, and I'm hoping to make a difference."

Since the creation of the ULI Terwilliger Center for Housing, ULI has released several publications related to housing affordability, including a series that documented the transportation and housing cost burden of workers in Boston, San Francisco, and Washington, D.C. Last year, ULI published the award-winning *Housing America's Workforce*, which showcases best practices in workforce and mixed-income housing development. The case studies in the book are recipients of the center's Jack Kemp Workforce Housing Models of Excellence Awards, named in remembrance of the former secretary of the U.S. Department of Housing and Urban Development, who served on the Terwilliger Center's advisory board. Earlier this year, the center released "America in 2013," the first in an annual series of research reports examining consumer preferences in housing, transportation, and communities. In addition, the center regularly convenes housing experts from the private, public, and nonprofit sectors to examine a range of housing issues and trends and discuss how best to catalyze development of mixed-income housing.

"Ron's level of involvement and his example of giving back are exceptional. Together, his industry expertise and passion for housing make him an incredibly effective advocate for a cause that is critical to improving the quality of life for people worldwide," says ULI chief executive officer Patrick L. Phillips. "He is a doer who is absolutely committed to making a measurable difference. Our Institute, our industry, and our communities have been made all the better for his leadership."

RHODE ISLAND ROW

A Mixed-Income Community Transforms a D.C. Neighborhood

At a February 2007 press conference at the National Press Club in downtown Washington, D.C., Ron Terwilliger announced the establishment of the ULI Terwilliger Center for Housing, saying, "I am committed to this because I believe in the urgency of expanding workforce housing. Everyone believes in providing decent housing when you ask the question, but no one wants people making less money living next to them. I believe our center can make a real difference in improving this unsatisfactory situation…. If we do not act now to bring housing and jobs closer together, we will seriously impede the ability of America's cities to compete with cities around the world."

A few miles away from that event, the eight-and-a-half acres next to the Rhode Island Avenue–Brentwood Metrorail station was a commuter parking lot; surrounded by declining neighborhoods, it was a bleak place to leave a car and catch a train. Now, just six years later, the site has been transformed into Rhode Island Row, a thriving 274-unit mixed-use community offering affordable, workforce, and market-rate apartments; 70,000 square feet of retail space; and upscale amenities, including outdoor fireplaces, a large outdoor wet bar and grills next to the pool, concierge services, a state-of-the-art fitness center, a green roof patio, and a sleek, thoughtfully appointed wood-and-glass community room with wi-fi access, comfortable lounging areas, large-screen televisions, a pool table, and an area for entertaining.

However, while all the perks hold considerable appeal, perhaps Rhode Island Row's biggest draw is convenience: the Metro station is just steps away. "I wanted to live here because I can walk across the street and be on the Metro," says community resident Melanie Clark, who moved into Rhode Island Row from a suburban neighborhood outside Baltimore. "Before [moving in], I did not have the same access to Washington. Living here has changed how I interact with the city. It's streamlined my life in a way that is fantastic."

The development, among the 2012 winners of the Terwilliger Center's Jack Kemp Workforce Housing Models of Excellence Awards, exemplifies Terwilliger's vision of mixed-income housing, which he considers the only viable solution to address the shortage of affordable housing near transit and employment hubs. The site, owned by the Washington Metropolitan Area Transit Authority (WMATA), is less than two miles from the city's central business district and only two stops from Union Station, a regional multimodal transportation hub. Its transformation from a parking lot into Rhode Island Row was made possible through a public/private partnership between WMATA and Bethesda, Maryland–based Urban Atlantic, which developed the community in a joint venture with A&R Development, with offices in Baltimore and Washington. Open just over a year, the community is 95 percent occupied; among the residents are D.C. police officers, Metro workers, teachers, and graduate students from area universities.

The approach to the development—from the financing to the amenities—reflects in large part Terwilliger's imprint on the career of Urban Atlantic president Vicki Davis, who worked at Trammell Crow Residential as a real estate developer in the mid-1980s and now serves on the Terwilliger Center's advisory board. "Ron was hugely influential," she says. "He indoctrinated the importance of only doing deals we knew would work and which were risk-adjusted for what we were producing. We also learned about using replicable design to hold down costs and the importance of providing great amenities and services."

Another lasting impact: during Davis's years at Trammell Crow Residential, the company developed some mixed-income housing, a relatively new concept at the time. "We learned that people with different incomes can live side by side without any knowledge by anyone that there is any significant difference," she says.

While Urban Atlantic's work ranges from the redevelopment of public housing to the development of luxury homes, its success in developing mixed-income communities (the company's Capitol Quarter, also in Washington, D.C., is another Kemp Award recipient) is a particular source of pride for Davis. "If you understand this business, you can make affordable housing work with the correct capital stack that offsets the expense. Knowing that it can be done is the first step. And it can be done." ∎

2014

Transforming Communities with the Resilience Dividend

Opposite: Shops and cafés along Walnut Street. "We wanted to signal that we were one community," Dr. Rodin says. *(Lipofsky.com)*

West Philadelphia's University City neighborhood is an active place, even between semesters at the University of Pennsylvania, the area's anchor institution. On an early August morning this past summer, people strolled along Walnut Street next to the university's campus, some stopping for coffee at one of several sidewalk cafés. Cyclists headed up and down Walnut's dedicated bike lanes. Shoppers were stocking up at the Fresh Grocer at Hamilton Square, and customers browsed in the university's expansive bookstore at University Square. Up and down the street, restaurants were gearing up for lunchtime.

With the start of Penn's 2014 fall semester still more than two weeks away, it's a safe bet that many of those who were milling about on Walnut that day are local residents and university employees. The stores and restaurants on Walnut are part of their community; these are the places they go to pick up groceries, meet friends, or just relax. And their neighborhood would soon be livened considerably by the 24–7 activity of Penn students who live in the neighborhood or who live on campus and consider the neighborhood an extension of the university.

The transition of Walnut Street from a boundary separating Penn from the city into a seam connecting the institution to the city is the result of an extraordinary effort set in motion nearly 20 years ago by Dr. Judith Rodin, now president of The Rockefeller Foundation and who served as president of the University of Pennsylvania from 1994 to 2004. Dr. Rodin's steadfast commitment to create positive change transformed Penn's relationship with the community, and it guides her current work in creating thriving communities around the world.

"My vision is a more resilient society—one where greater opportunity is shared by more people," Dr. Rodin says. "Throughout my life and career, it has always mattered to me that people feel empowered to participate in decision making—in outcomes that affect their lives. And my work enables that vision to be actualized."

"My vision is a more resilient society—one where greater opportunity is shared by more people. Throughout my life and career, it has always mattered to me that people feel empowered to participate in decision making—in outcomes that affect their lives."

PHILADELPHIA, PA DR. JUDITH RODIN • 2014 NICHOLS LAUREATE

Left: Sports fields and a public park were among the revitalization projects on the east side of the Penn campus. "Judy understood that what is good for Penn should be good for the community, and what is good for the community should be good for Penn," says Laurie Olin, partner at OLIN and a professor of practice at Penn. *(Lipofsky.com)*

Right: The Penn Bookstore at 36th and Walnut is located on what had been a parking lot for more than 30 years. *(Lipofsky.com)*

The tremendous positive impact Dr. Rodin has made on people's lives globally—starting with one university neighborhood—has earned her the 2014 Urban Land Institute J.C. Nichols Prize for Visionaries in Urban Development. The institute's highest honor, the Nichols Prize recognizes a person, or a person representing an institution, who has demonstrated a longtime commitment to the creation of communities that prosper by providing a high quality of life for all residents and which reflect the highest standards of design and development. The $100,000 prize honors the legacy of Kansas City, Missouri, developer J.C. Nichols, a founding ULI member considered to be one of America's most innovative entrepreneurs in land use during the first half of the 20th century.

"The Nichols prize exemplifies people who have made a difference in their community, and Dr. Rodin has done that extremely well," says Nichols Prize jury member Mark Johnson, president of Civitas, an urban design and landscape architecture firm in Denver. "She has shown a career-long commitment to breaking barriers and changing perceptions about how to improve a community."

"Dr. Rodin is on the leading edge of community building," notes Nichols Prize jury chair James D. Klingbeil, chairman and chief executive officer of Klingbeil Capital Management Ltd., a national real estate investment and management company based in San Francisco. "Her trial by fire came while she was at Penn, and she took that experience and has applied it very successfully at The Rockefeller Foundation."

• • •

When Dr. Rodin came to the University of Pennsylvania, the neighborhoods surrounding Penn were unkempt, crime ridden, and forbidding. Walnut Street was marked by desolate parking lots and a dilapidated strip center. Penn bused students to the downtown Center City district to shop. The university buildings faced inward; loading docks were the main contact point with the city streets. Walking off campus was unpleasant during the day and considered dangerous after dark.

The situation was intolerable for Dr. Rodin, both as the university president and as a native of West Philadelphia who had grown up in the area when it still thrived. The deplorable state of the neighborhood was undercutting Penn's ability to recruit world-caliber faculty and students; and, although the university was Philadelphia's largest employer, its location was increasingly being viewed as an impediment to future growth and competitiveness.

In 1996, the circumstances became even grimmer when, over the course of a few weeks, one student was killed and others were mugged next to the campus boundary—a series of tragic events that forced Penn to take immediate action. Rather than retreat further from the community, Dr. Rodin chose a decidedly different course. "We could have built a higher wall, but the solution that started with Judy [Dr. Rodin] was that we needed to stop being apart from the neighborhood and start being part of it," says Egbert Perry, a trustee of the University of Pennsylvania and chairman and chief executive officer of Atlanta-based Integral, a real estate development, advisory, and investment management company.

"Universities and medical centers are often the unwitting contributors to a neighborhood's deterioration—they need more space, and as they push further into the neighborhoods, they drive people out. I really wanted to turn us [Penn] into an engine for good," Dr. Rodin says. "We understood that we could not do this to the neighborhood, or even for the neighborhood, but that we had to do it with the neighborhood. The best design and the greatest architecture are insufficient without community engagement."

What began as an urgent measure by Penn to create a safer environment for the students evolved into a full-scale neighborhood revitalization—a movement both gutsy and unproven. Known as the West Philadelphia Initiatives (WPI), the strategy was designed as an interlocking series of programs to address the area's security, education, housing, and economic development needs, with the university taking the lead role as developer and facilitator. Incentives were created to encourage faculty and staff members to live near the university. With each phase of redevelopment, the university's insularity was replaced with a solidarity of school and community.

"Judy would not only strategize, but would get out, sit with community members, and refine what we were doing by listening to them and learning from them," recalls John Fry, who served as an executive vice president in Dr. Rodin's administration and is now president of Drexel University in Philadelphia. "The more we got into it, the more we realized that the job was much larger than we had initially anticipated. But through it all, she was undaunted; she was fearless."

Ultimately, the university solved its security problem through urban design. "We said, 'This isn't about keeping kids out of the neighborhood. This is about how we light the streets and sidewalks, how we open the university buildings to the street.' We wanted to signal that we were one community," Dr. Rodin says.

• • •

A quote from Eleanor Roosevelt is engraved over the interior entrance to the Penn Bookstore at 36th Street and Walnut: "You must do the thing you think you cannot do." It sums up the philosophy that drove the revitalization, which started with moving the university's bookstore out of the basement of a campus building and into a 55,000-square-foot space across the street. The store, located on what had been a parking lot for more than 30 years, opened in 1998 not just as a place to buy textbooks, but as a full-service bookstore with a café.

The Inn at Penn hotel, located next door, occupies the upper floors of the building; the bookstore-hotel project was the university's first mixed-use venture as part of the WPI. In the ensuing years, Penn kept the momentum going on the west side of the campus with the development of the grocery store and the addition of more retail and dining space, a cinema, student housing, a 700-car parking garage, and a beautifully designed public elementary school. The university then shifted its focus to the campus's east side, acquiring and converting an old industrial building into apartments, retail space, and office space, as well as building research, medical, and engineering facilities, plus playing fields and a public park.

Laurie Olin, partner at Olin, a landscape architecture, urban design, and planning firm with studios in Philadelphia and Los Angeles, and a professor of practice at Penn, had taught at the university for nearly 20 years before Dr. Rodin's arrival. "Judy understood that what is good for Penn should be good for the community, and what is good for the community should be good for Penn," Olin says. "She understood that the university needed a soft edge, it needed to be part of the community, not a thing next to it."

"[Dr. Rodin] has shown a career-long commitment to breaking barriers and changing perceptions about how to improve a community."

MARK JOHNSON • 2014 JURY MEMBER

"Judy was committed to creating an environment that encouraged students to be engaged citizens, and she realized that you cannot talk about civic engagement and then build facilities that disrupt or do not interact with the neighborhood," explains Omar Blaik, co-chief executive officer at U3 Advisors, a real estate and economic development consulting practice in Philadelphia, and a senior executive in Penn's facilities and real estate department during Dr. Rodin's tenure. "We needed to add [land] uses that were not about us, but about the community."

In addition to the hundreds of millions of dollars Penn invested in commercial development, housing, and public space along the Walnut Street corridor, the university built the Sadie Tanner Mossell Alexander University of Pennsylvania Partnership School (Alexander earned five degrees from Penn between 1918 and 1974, including the nation's first PhD awarded to an African American and the first law degree awarded to a female student at Penn). Known as the Penn Alexander Elementary School, it is a neighborhood school operated by the Philadelphia School District in cooperation with Penn's Graduate School of Education. The construction of the school provided an incentive for faculty and staff members to live in University City, but it ultimately benefited the greater community—Dr. Rodin insisted that it be a public school open to all neighborhood residents (about 75 percent of the school's students have no Penn affiliations).

The addition of the school proved as pivotal in forging ties with the community as the commercial development projects, notes Blaik, who moved to the neighborhood and whose children attended Penn Alexander. "The school was a way for people with the university to relate to the neighborhood residents. When your kids all go to the same school, it creates a strong bond," he says. "Your personal goals coincide with those of your neighbors. It creates an organic blurring of who is us and who is them."

In 2003, the West Philadelphia Initiatives won an Award for Excellence from ULI; in 2004, Dr. Rodin was the first female to win the Greater Philadelphia Chamber of Commerce's William Penn Award, which recognizes personal, professional, and community contributions to the Greater Philadelphia region. The movement has had staying power; despite changes in the university's leadership, Penn is still building projects based on the revitalization plan.

The Sadie Tanner Mossell Alexander University of Pennsylvania Partnership School. Built by the university, it is a neighborhood school operated by the Philadelphia School District in cooperation with Penn's Graduate School of Education. The addition of the school proved as pivotal in forging ties with the community as the commercial projects. (Lipofsky.com)

Says university trustee Perry: "It was bold, because it was about investing in the neighborhood, not on the campus proper. That was new territory for the trustees. . . . [But] it has truly caused the transformation of the university and the life around it, which is great for recruiting students." Applications have risen so much that only about 12 percent of Penn's applicants are now accepted, compared with 50 percent in 1993, and the university's endowment has increased nearly fivefold to its current level of about $7.7 billion. "I don't think any one of us [Penn trustees] thinks this is something that has passed its time, because it continues to pays dividends every day," Perry says.

Fry, the Drexel president, is applying the lessons learned at Penn by leading Drexel's revival of neighborhoods around that university. "I am paying her [Dr. Rodin] the best tribute I could pay her, which is to extend the ethos, to carry on the work," he says.

. . .

Etched in glass at the entrance to The Rockefeller Foundation's headquarters in New York City is the phrase "Innovation for the Next 100 Years." With an endowment of more than $4 billion, the foundation is one of the largest philanthropic organizations in the world. Established by John D. Rockefeller Sr. in 1913, its 100-year history reflects countless achievements that fulfill the mission set by its founder, which is to support the well-being of humanity around the globe. The foundation's past work includes providing support for the development of a vaccine against yellow fever; for Jane Jacobs's efforts to redefine urban planning and design; for the Green Revolution in farming, which increased crop production in developing countries; and for the Mother to Child Transmission Plus Initiative, which focuses on caring for HIV-positive women and their families and preventing transmitting the virus from mother to child. The foundation has supported the work of more than 220 Nobel laureates, and two of its own officers have received Nobel prizes.

When Dr. Rodin assumed the foundation presidency in 2005, she applied two lessons learned from her community building experience at Penn—the value of (1) leveraging and (2) partnerships as ways to maximize outcomes. Over the past eight years, the annual

"YOU MUST DO THE THING
YOU THINK YOU CANNOT DO."
ELEANOR ROOSEVELT

amount awarded by the foundation has risen to approximately $200 million in grants, which have leveraged more than $1 billion in additional funds from partners during that time. "The message I brought to Rockefeller is that it really isn't sufficient to just give grants. To have a huge transformational impact, you really need to leverage your resources effectively," she says. "Rockefeller is now viewed as an institution not only with an unbelievable storied 100-year history of enormous impact in many places, but an institution that is on the leading edge of innovation by thinking strategically about both leverage and partnerships."

Applying the same pioneering approach she used at Penn, Dr. Rodin has overseen a structural shift at the foundation that has resulted in a portfolio of interconnected initiatives. Each initiative addresses multiple focus areas, all aimed at meeting four equally important goals: revalue ecosystems, advance health, secure livelihoods, and transform cities. Specifically, the initiatives are aimed at creating new job opportunities for youth in Africa and the United States; bringing clean electrification to rural villages in India; developing the fields of impact investing and innovative finance; advancing access to universal health coverage in developing countries; and building more-resilient communities and cities.

All of the focus areas are part of an overarching effort to reinforce the resilience of communities to environmental, economic, and social changes—enabling them to realize what the foundation refers to as the "resilience dividend." The term, which is the title of a new book by Dr. Rodin, is one she often uses to describe the benefits of proactive investments in resilience building. "Resilience is about planning, it's about investing in ways that are protective," she explains. "As we see this work unfolding, we are beginning to understand that there is a dividend, even in the good times, for investing in resilience. It provides more economic opportunities and better social cohesion. It's not just for the prevention of that horrible thing that may happen. . . . We believe strongly that building resilience can reduce the likelihood that every disruption becomes a disaster. And if you think about it that way, it really is a good metaphor for what we are trying to accomplish, and I think people are getting it."

"Judy has built on the 20th-century innovations of The Rockefeller Foundation to create an entirely new paradigm for the 21st century," says Ford Foundation president Darren Walker, who served as a vice president at The Rockefeller Foundation from 2005 to 2010. "She has created a new way of thinking about cities and the urban landscape through this notion of the resilience dividend. It takes into consideration the multiple outcomes that can be associated with a smart investment on the front end.

"That is the way Judy approaches things, in terms of how to get the biggest bang from an investment, how to solve a problem using limited resources. Judy is very smart about how to strategically deploy resources to get the greatest impact."

· · ·

In May 2013, The Rockefeller Foundation announced the "100 Resilient Cities Challenge," a $100 million commitment to build resilience in cities around the world. The foundation defines resilience as "the capacity of individuals, communities, institutions, businesses, and systems within a city to survive, adapt, and grow no matter what kinds of

Opposite:

Top: A quote from Eleanor Roosevelt, engraved over the interior entrance of the Penn Bookstore, sums up the philosophy that drove the University City neighborhood revitalization. *(Lipofsky.com)*

Bottom right: Dr. Rodin celebrates with Nigerian farm women at The Rockefeller Foundation's centennial event on agriculture in Abuja, Nigeria, in July 2013. *(The Rockefeller Foundation)*

Bottom left: The Rave Movie Theater at 40th and Walnut. "Judy . . . realized that you cannot talk about civic engagement and then build facilities that disrupt or do not interact with the neighborhood," explains Omar Blaik, co-chief executive officer at U3 Advisors, who was a senior executive in the Penn Facilities and Real Estate Services department during Dr. Rodin's tenure. *(Lipofsky.com)*

chronic stresses and acute shocks they experience." Through the program, grants are being awarded to 100 cities to support the hiring of a chief resilience officer, as well as to assist with the creation and implementation of a resilience strategy.

In December 2013, 32 cities ranging from Byblos, Lebanon, to New Orleans were selected from the first funding round as grant recipients; an additional 33 recipients from the second round will be announced within a few months. The two funding rounds collectively drew more than 700 applications, which Dr. Rodin proudly points to as an indicator that cities worldwide are "thinking about resilience is a very deliberative way." Local officials in cities that have already received grants are citing the positive impact of having a chief resilience officer who is integrated across all elements of municipal government, she notes.

In a testimonial posted on the foundation's 100 Resilient Cities website (www.100resilientcities.org), New Orleans Mayor Mitchell J. Landrieu says, "The Rockefeller Foundation's partnership is invaluable to mayors across the world because it is critical to our ability to identify and create innovative solutions on the ground. Through this collaboration, I am confident that New Orleans will become the global model for resilience by our city's 300th anniversary in 2018, building resiliency across all sectors and identifying the best approaches to our city's inherited natural challenges."

"Judy's focus on urban transformation, on cities as a place of opportunity, and on increasing equity for citizens and others emigrating to cities, is really fundamental to where The Rockefeller Foundation is going with its programs," says Nichols Prize jury member Marilyn J. Taylor, dean of the University of Pennsylvania's School of Design. "Being named one of the [100 Resilient] cities means receiving a commitment from the foundation to work with the stakeholders in each city to assemble the resources, leverage assets, and get to implementation. Judy truly gets things done."

The foundation is the lead supporter of Rebuild by Design, a program created by the federal government in response to Hurricane Sandy's devastation in 2012 of communities in the Northeast region of the United States. Rebuild by Design is dedicated to creating innovative community- and policy-based solutions to protect the nation's cities that are most vulnerable to increasingly intense weather events and other environmental uncertainties. While the program to date has focused on areas affected by Sandy, it is being expanded to communities across the United States.

Initiated by the U.S. Department of Housing and Urban Development (HUD) and the Presidential Hurricane Sandy Rebuilding Task Force, Rebuild by Design involves a design competition through which winning teams of researchers and designers work with local businesses, policy makers, and other stakeholders on redeveloping their communities to be environmentally and economically sound. In the program's first phase, ten interdisciplinary teams were selected in 2013 to participate in a yearlong process and competition; the teams include architects, landscape architects, regional and transportation planners, engineers, and community organizers.

On June 2, 2014, then-HUD Secretary Shaun Donovan announced the winning proposals, which offered redevelopment schemes for Staten Island, the Bronx, Long Island, and Manhattan in New York and Hoboken and the Meadowlands in New Jersey.

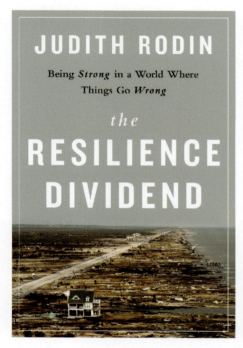

The Resilience Dividend, a new book by Dr. Rodin, documents the benefits of proactively investing in community resilience. "We are beginning to understand that there is a dividend . . . for investing in resilience. It provides more economic opportunities and better social cohesion," she says. *(The Rockefeller Foundation)*

Dr. Rodin at The Rockefeller Foundation's Centennial event on health in Beijing, China, in January 2013. "At The Rockefeller Foundation, we dream of a world in which globalization's benefits are more equitably shared and the inevitable challenges that accompany this much dynamism and volatility are more easily weathered by building greater resilience," she said in her remarks. *(The Rockefeller Foundation)*

Although the specifics of each plan were tailored for the designated areas, Dr. Rodin points out that land use planning was the design element at the core of all the proposals. "Land use is a fundamental pillar of building a resilient city," she says. "If we get land use planning wrong, we cannot get transportation planning right or energy [conservation] right. . . . A resilient city relies on how the land is thought about and designed."

The foundation is expanding its focus on resilience with a new program aimed at helping the most vulnerable areas of the world recoup more of the funds spent on disaster recovery and leverage more funds for development. Together with the United States Agency for International Development and other partners, the foundation is supporting initiatives in the Sahel and Horn regions of Africa and the region between South and Southeast Asia to enable humanitarian relief agencies to invest more in building capacity before emergencies. "We are picking the hardest spots to push this idea forward," Dr. Rodin says. "Resilience applies to how you organize leadership and governance and to the kind of social fabric and social cohesion that exists, as well as physical infrastructure, land use planning, and design. All of that together is what really creates this resilient capacity that we have been emphasizing.

"Resilience is often referred to as an inborn quality, but we are learning that resilience is a learnable characteristic for people, institutions, and cities. If we keep at this—we at Rockefeller and the global community in general—we can acquire the skills to build resilience into our land use planning, our architecture and design, our school-based curricula—all the many ways that enable it to be taught and learned. That gives me great hope."

NICHOLS PRIZE JURIES

2000

Robert C. Larson, *Jury Chair*
Vice Chairman, Taubman Centers Inc.

Robert Campbell
Architecture Critic, Boston Globe

Alex Krieger
*Chairman, Graduate School of Design
Harvard University*

Harvey Gantt
Partner, Gantt Huberman Architects

Jaquelin T. Robertson
Partner, Cooper, Robertson & Partners

2001

Robert C. Larson, *Jury Chair*
*Chairman, Lazard Freres Real Estate
Investors LLC*

Paul Goldberger
Architecture Critic, New Yorker

Alex Krieger
*Chairman, Graduate School of Design
Harvard University*

Harvey Gantt
Partner, Gantt Huberman Architects

Jaquelin T. Robertson
Principal, Cooper, Robertson & Partners

2002

Robert C. Larson, *Jury Chair*
*Chairman, Lazard Freres Real Estate
Investors LLC*

Joseph E. Brown
*President and Chief Executive Officer,
EDAW Inc.*

Adele Chatfield-Taylor
President, American Academy in Rome

Paul Goldberger
Architecture Critic, New Yorker

Peter Rummell
*Chairman and Chief Executive Officer,
St. Joe Company*

2003

Peter Rummell, *Jury Chair*
*Chairman and Chief Executive Officer,
St. Joe Company*

Joseph E. Brown
*President and Chief Executive Officer,
EDAW Inc.*

Adele Chatfield-Taylor
President, American Academy in Rome

Paul Goldberger
Architecture Critic, New Yorker

James A. Ratner
*Executive Vice President, Forest City
Enterprises Inc.*

2004

Peter Rummell, *Jury Chair*
*Chairman and Chief Executive Officer,
St. Joe Company*

Joseph E. Brown
*President and Chief Executive Officer,
EDAW Inc.*

Robert Campbell
Architecture Critic, Boston Globe

A. Eugene Kohn
President, Kohn Pedersen Fox

Ronald Ratner
*Executive Vice President and Director,
Forest City Enterprises Inc.*

2005

Joseph E. Brown, *Jury Chair*
*President and Chief Executive Officer,
EDAW Inc.*

Robert Campbell
Fellow, American Institute of Architects

Bonnie Fisher
Principal, ROMA Design Group

A. Eugene Kohn
President, Kohn Pedersen Fox

Christopher B. Leinberger
Founding Partner, Arcadia Land Company

2006

A. Eugene Kohn, *Jury Chair*
Chairman, Kohn Pedersen Fox

Robert Campbell
Fellow, American Institute of Architects

Bonnie Fisher
Principal, ROMA Design Group

Christopher B. Leinberger
Founding Partner, Arcadia Land Company

Jeremy Newsum
*Chief Executive and Trustee,
Grosvenor Estate*

2007

Jeremy Newsum, *Jury Chair*
*Chief Executive and Trustee,
Grosvenor Estate*

Bonnie Fisher
Principal, ROMA Design Group

Christopher B. Leinberger
Founding Partner, Arcadia Land Company

Witold Rybczynski
Martin and Margy Meyerson Professor of Urbanism, University of Pennsylvania

Paul Schell
Former Mayor, City of Seattle

2008

Jeremy Newsum, *Jury Chair*
Chief Executive and Trustee, Grosvenor Estate

Elizabeth Plater-Zyberk
Founding Partner, Duany Plater-Zyberk & Company

Deborah Ratner Salzberg
President, Forest City Washington Inc.

Witold Rybczynski
Martin and Margy Meyerson Professor of Urbanism, University of Pennsylvania

Paul Schell
Former Mayor, City of Seattle

2009

James M. DeFrancia, *Jury Chair*
President, Lowe Enterprises Community Development

Todd W. Mansfield
Chairman and Chief Executive Officer, Crosland

Elizabeth Plater-Zyberk
Founding Partner, Duany Plater-Zyberk & Company

Witold Rybczynski
Martin and Margy Meyerson Professor of Urbanism, University of Pennsylvania

Paul Schell
Former Mayor, City of Seattle

2010

James M. DeFrancia, *Jury Chair*
President, Lowe Enterprises Community Development

Neal Peirce
Chairman, Citistates Group

Elizabeth Plater-Zyberk
Founding Partner, Duany Plater-Zyberk & Company

Judith Rodin
President, Rockefeller Foundation

Deborah Ratner Salzberg
President, Forest City Washington Inc.

2011

James M. DeFrancia, *Jury Chair*
President, Lowe Enterprises Inc.

Ronald A. Altoon
Partner, Altoon & Porter Architects LLP

F. Barton Harvey III
Former Chairman and Chief Executive Officer, Enterprise Community Partners

Neal Peirce
Chairman, Citistates Group

Deborah Ratner Salzberg
President, Forest City Washington Inc.

2012

John Bucksbaum, *Jury Chair*
Founder, Bucksbaum Retail Properties LLC

Ronald A. Altoon
Founding Design Partner, Altoon Partners LLP

F. Barton Harvey III
Former Chairman and Chief Executive Officer, Enterprise Community Partners

James D. Klingbeil
Chairman and Chief Executive Officer, Klingbeil Capital Management

David M. Schwarz
President and Chief Executive Officer, David M. Schwarz Architects

2013

John Bucksbaum, *Jury Chair*
Founder, Bucksbaum Retail Properties LLC

Ronald A. Altoon
Founding Design Partner, Altoon Partners LLP

F. Barton Harvey III
Former Chairman and Chief Executive Officer, Enterprise Community Partners

James D. Klingbeil
Chairman and Chief Executive Officer, Klingbeil Capital Management

Marilyn Jordan Taylor
Dean and Paley Professor, University of Pennsylvania School of Design

2014

James D. Klingbeil, *Jury Chair*
Chairman and Chief Executive Officer,
Klingbeil Capital Management

John Bucksbaum
Founder, Bucksbaum Retail Properties LLC

Mark Johnson
President, Civitas

Marilyn Jordan Taylor
Dean and Paley Professor, University of
Pennsylvania School of Design

Sir Stuart Lipton
Lipton Rogers Developments LLP

Joseph E. Brown
Chief Innovation Officer, AECOM
2007–

Kay N. Callison
Miller Nichols Charitable Foundation
2000–

Peter Calthorpe
President, Calthorpe Associates
2000–2005

Robert Davis
Partner, Arcadia Land Company
2000–2012

James M. DeFrancia
Principal, Lowe Enterprises Inc.
2000–

Ken Fligg
Nichols Family Trust
2000

Harrison Fraker
Professor of Architecture and Urban
Design, College of Environmental Design,
University of California, Berkeley
2013–

Lizanne Galbreath
Managing Partner, Galbreath & Company
2012–

David Howard
Executive Vice President, Development
and Foundation, Urban Land Institute
2014–

Doug S. Kelbaugh
Professor of Architecture and Urban
Planning, Taubman College of Architecture
and Urban Planning, University of Michigan
2000–

Todd W. Mansfield
Chief Executive Officer, Crescent
Communities
2006–2013

Jeannette Nichols
Miller Nichols Charitable Foundation
2000–

Susan Nichols
Nichols Agency
2013–

Wayne Nichols
Nichols Agency
2000–

Diana B. Permar
President, Permar Inc.
2000–2005

Patrick L. Phillips
Global Chief Executive Officer,
Urban Land Institute
2006–

Clarence Roeder
Former Vice President, J.C. Nichols Company
2000–2005

Richard M. Rosan
Former President, ULI Foundation
2000–2014

Jonathan F.P. Rose
President, Jonathan Rose Companies
2000–2005, 2007–2012

James W. Todd
President, The Peterson Companies
2000–2005

Smedes York
President, York Companies
2000–